DEMASS

DEMASS

Transforming the Dinosaur Corporation

M.M. Stuckey

Publisher's Message by
Norman Bodek

Productivity Press
Cambridge, Massachusetts   Norwalk, Connecticut

Productivity Press
P.O. Box 3007
Cambridge, Massachusetts 02140
United States of America
Telephone: (617) 497-5146
Telefax: (617) 868-3524

Cover design by Gary Ragaglia
Printed and bound by Maple-Vail Book Manufacturing Group
Manufactured in the United States of America on acid-free paper

Library of Congress Cataloging-in-Publication Data

Stuckey, M.M.
Demass: transforming the dinosaur corporation/M.M. Stuckey.
p. cm.
Includes bibliographical references and index.
ISBN 1-56327-042-0
1. Decentralization in management — United States. 2. Small business — United States. 3. Management information systems. I. Title.
HD50.S783 1993
658.4'02 — dc20 92-28998
CIP

93 94 95 10 9 8 7 6 5 4 3 2 1

America's great manufacturing companies, which grew to be multinational giants and prospered by becoming bigger and better than their competitors, should cherish yesterday, but start demassifying today — or prepare for extinction tomorrow!

Contents

After all is said and done, there is only one important measure of a good business idea — the bottom line. Smart goal setting, organizational revitalization through demassification, and consistent measurement of what a company is trying to manage will improve today's results and give a company the flexibility it will surely need to survive and thrive tomorrow.

Companies and their managements do not improve by doing the comfortable thing. They progress by facing challenges squarely and adapting to them as they would to an approaching wave. A big wave is drawing near to American business. The choice is clear: learn to surf (demassify), or prepare to wipe out.

Publisher's Message

M. M. Stuckey, past senior line executive at several *Fortune* 500 companies in America, draws on his experience of working at the top of mammoth organizations in this latest of Productivity's publications: *Demass: Transforming the Dinosaur Corporation*. Currently founder and CEO of FOURTH SHIFT Corporation, he offers in this book both methodological and technical solutions to the stagnation plaguing America's corporate industrial empires.

Demassification, a word Stuckey coined, cuts through the structural inflexibility and sluggish communications of massive organizations with a two-edged sword: structural reorganization into small business units and local management empowerment through client/server software and systems that provide immediate access to information where and when it is needed.

Why is demassification a critical message today? Americans have always believed bigger was better. Who would have dreamed that anyone could compete against giant firms like GM, GE, RCA, Pan Am, IBM? Companies like these, who cornered such large shares of the American market, until recently have had only the fear of becoming monopolies standing in the way of unhindered growth. They have had to artificially curb their expansion to defer government intervention.

But in the last decade the Japanese have proven that big is not necessarily better; and smaller capital-short American companies are proving the value of greater innovation and speed to market. Massive firms are staying alive by buying smaller ones in order to gain innovation they have ceased to be able to produce themselves.

> Of the 100 firms heading *Fortune*'s first list of America's 500 biggest companies, published in 1956, only 29 can still be found in the top 100 of its latest list, published on April 1st. Of the 100 biggest non-American firms listed in 1956, only 27 were still there in 1989, the last time the magazine published such a list. Within the span of one working life, well over two-thirds of the world's biggest companies were jostled out of the way by faster-growing firms. (*The Economist*, April 4, 1992, p. 15)

The big "dinosaur corporations" can no longer operate efficiently in the rapid-change environment of current global markets. They can no longer respond adequately where fast response and flexibility are necessary to survive. Survival (let alone market leadership) goes again and again to the smaller companies who have such flexibility.

Stuckey addresses the executives of America's giant organizations with a message they must hear: in order to sustain themselves they must demassify! And Productivity is pleased to publish this message because it rings true to the understanding we have always brought to our readers' attention: total participation and local empowerment are the factors critical to business survival in today's markets.

Upon examination of Stuckey's message, demass may seem like a dangerous solution. A CEO needs a lot of trust to reorganize and empower, and very little trust seems to exist in organizations that have grown to such proportions by the efforts of a few leaders at the top. How do such powerful leaders learn to let go; to trust their managers and support them; to let others do the job they have always done themselves? This is certainly not an easy message to absorb. And Stuckey's message is only the beginning of the thought process. It raises the essential questions, and provides some thoughtful answers. The hope of this book is to cause the essential questions to be addressed. Each organization will have to find its own way on the demassification journey. Productivity looks forward to sharing the experiences and supporting the change of those American giants who accept the challenge to demassify.

We wish to thank Dorothy Lohmann as managing editor for her excellent efforts with the manuscript, Laura St. Clair for preparation of the manuscript for production, David Lennon, Gayle Joyce, Susan Cobb, and Karla Tolbert for their contributions to the design and composition of the book, Jennifer Cross for the index, and Gary Ragaglia for the cover design.

Norman Bodek
President

Diane Asay
Series Editor

Acknowledgments

Few books are the work of a single person. In this project I benefited from the help, counsel, and encouragement of many, but several must be mentioned individually. I wish to thank Paul Halvorson, who served as project manager through the writing of this book, making the connections and managing the schedule; Jim Lahner, who helped with research; Michael Finley, who helped with his editorial comments and good humor; Jack Philbin and George Hannye, both of whose ground-breaking efforts at Eastman Kodak helped codify this whole concept of demassification; Diane Asay for her work improving the manuscript; and Bob Price, retired CEO and chairman of Control Data Corporation, who has provided me with incisive wisdom and helpful advice.

For my wife, Lee — intelligent,
caring and supportive.
Loved by many.
Especially me.

Introduction

Demassification, or *demass* for short, is an unfamiliar word, and busy executives like things netted out, up-front. So here, in a nutshell, is what it means and why it's a vital survival strategy for most large corporations.

Based upon what I have seen, I have become convinced that sheer mass and overcentralization are the twin nemeses of most large multinational corporations. There is no better current example of the pitfalls of centralized controls than the last days of the Soviet Union. Inefficient and out of touch with the needs of its people across its far-flung empire, the nation collapsed inwardly, breaking into over a dozen smaller pieces. Heaven knows the Soviet Union had lots of problems, but there was one main reason it didn't *work*: as an organization, it was rooted in command and control from a single central point of a vast population, with an extraordinary collection of problems that changed almost daily.

Less dramatically but quite similarly, centralization isn't working for scores of large multinational corporations, either. Trotting out the usual remedy, *corporate decentralization*, doesn't seem to alter the landscape much.

As I see it, corporate decentralization is a sham, a masquerade. It is supposed to break down a large company into smaller, more workable units, but in fact it seldom does. Instead of a single all-powerful CEO or management committee, decentralization results in a half-dozen or so sub-CEOs or sub-management committees, all still pursuing the same original basic goals of centralized command and control, *but now they are in charge!* Decentralization doesn't work because it doesn't change what needs to be changed.

Demass at least holds the promise to change what needs to be changed. That change is delegation of command and control from the center, to small teams of workers, or independent business units — *a democratization of organization.*

I define demassification as *radical* decentralization, *grass-roots* decentralization, with maximum autonomy delegated down to the small business-unit level, with attendant downsizing of information-processing technology. Radical, because it is a voluntary diminution of personal power by executives manning the central helm. Grass roots, because it truly builds power throughout the ranks of the organization.

Demassification is decentralization brought down to the intimate, hands-on, small-team level. It is the purest form of empowerment.

Demass can transform a large corporation into a "street of shops," where the people in each business unit are empowered and equipped with the tools and information they need to maximize service, productivity, and profitability. In a demassified company, departments are transformed from functional units into business units, and each business unit includes all the functions required to succeed in that business. The corporation may still be massive on paper, but it has changed. It is no longer a giant super-fortress that takes two miles of runway for takeoff, hopelessly bad at dodging incoming enemy missiles. Now it is a disciplined squadron of high-speed fighters, each with an intelligent, empowered pilot.

Operating under many roofs instead of one, the demassified company's top executives now can scrutinize more objectively each unit's purpose and performance. Can a unit's particular job be done more efficiently and with less outside investment? Where is new investment most justified? What is strategic and what is just here because it's always been here? Where are the quality and time-to-market bottlenecks? Where is the real profit being produced? Where is the real pain?

Demassified organizations work better because they are in better harmony with what turns people on!

People want to feel challenged. They want to contribute in *their* way. They want to be told "atta-boy" and "atta-girl" when they get the job done. They want to feel they have some control over what they are working on, even if the boss gets to call the shots on what the goals and ground rules are. Employees want to be paid well, yes, but more than anything they want to enjoy what they do all day long. They want to be proud of themselves.

One underpinning for the success of any demassified entity is information — getting it fast and accurately. When getting needed operational information takes too long or is too difficult, everyone gets frustrated, and quality and time-to-market head south. And then the finger-pointing begins.

Therefore, vital operating information and effective information-processing tools must be at the fingertips of the people managing and working in each business unit. Instead of having to serve at the altar of *centralized* accounting, *centralized* purchasing, and *centralized* management information systems (sometimes called MIS), each business unit should have its own accountants, purchasers, and information systems people. Workers in business units should have their own information-processing systems and tools.

All business units must communicate their operating financials as well as work input requirements and product output data to internal and external trading partners. The key is that information flows internally and outward rather than predominantly upward.

Demassification has obviously attractive goals. The CEO of any major corporation would give both eye teeth to have all department heads and first-level workers charged up and strongly motivated to give their company their best efforts. But the reason demass is a new option is that it was not achievable until recently.

The massive corporation is a creature of the postwar, mainframe computer mentality. Where mainframe number crunching made the supercorporation possible, today's microtechnology-based, user-friendly distributed computing systems make possible a more localized, more intimate, more interactive version of that supercorporation.

Think of demassification as a rope made of two braided strands. The first strand is *organizational restructuring*; the second is the *downsizing of information-processing technology*.

Organizational restructuring to achieve demassification requires transferring significant power and prerogatives down to the business-unit level. It requires developing and using new ways of thinking, different ways of leading, and different ways of measuring performance at every management level, all the way up to the offices of the president and chief executive officer. It will result in fewer levels of management, thus more candidates for business-unit line management jobs.

The other strand, downsizing of information-processing technology, is necessary to provide demassified organizations the individualized control over information needed to get business-unit-driven work done rapidly and with dominion over the timing and content of what gets done.

Taken individually, neither strand will provide a rope strong enough for a giant multinational corporation to pull itself above the enormous difficulties it is encountering now, or will be encountering soon. But braided together, they can form a powerful lifeline to a new type of company: a corporation giant in size yet capable of understanding its component parts, capable of trimming off cancerous parts before they invade vital organs, capable of responding rapidly to new technologies and moving customer requirements and narrowing market segmentation — a giant corporation with employees who are excited about their work.

The change can be rejuvenating, especially for overworked, overstressed, and often underappreciated CEOs. They may enjoy seeing that reportedly vanished, old-time work ethic at work again. They may even rediscover the joy of achievement that brought them into business in the first place.

1
Manuphobia

American manufacturing is in trouble. A root cause is manuphobia, the executive fear that he or she can never understand or affect what goes on down in manufacturing. So executives set a course that feels about right. They keep their distance from what is going on in operations and grimace at the results.

Pete Bates, the CEO of America's 82nd largest industrial company, sits behind his great mahogany desk. His family smiles up at him from a framed photo. At least *they're* in a good mood, he says to himself, rubbing his tired eyes.

Today's bad news: another of his company's top customers has just announced separate major contracts with Japanese and German competitors. Haven't these people heard of the "Buy American" campaign?

At last month's shareholders, meeting, his observations had been upbeat, stressing that profits were up and that the company's two-year-old "Quality First" program was really starting to show results. He had the crowd in the palm of his hand. People came up to him later and slapped him on the back. "Hey, that was just terrific!" everyone said. He wished he felt as good as his speeches sounded.

Today, sales are up and quality has improved dramatically. But on his desk is a confidential analysis, and the news is sobering: it shows that their highest grossing, most profitable product line is losing domestic market share to Japanese imports, and while product quality has improved a lot, it's just catching up to the competition's quality of two years ago.

This isn't good news, but what worries him most is that, throughout the company, new product introductions are slowing down. His company can't seem to grind it out anymore.

Two years ago he and his top executives sat in on critical product meetings, where the research and development team presented pictures, slides, and models of great next-generation products that everyone was sure would knock the socks off the competition. Today, these products due for introduction about now are at least 18 months behind schedule. He closes his eyes and mutters a curse through clenched teeth: *18 months!*

These new products are precisely what sales is crying out for, right now, today! Waiting 18 more months means sure disaster. In fact, sales has already issued competitive reports saying that more than 20 additional enhancements are needed on this new product line if it is to keep up with the competition's expected improvements. But research and development pointed out that to try such mid-course enhancements, before the product is even out, will obliterate whatever confidence in delivery dates they still have.

Seeing rising internal manufacturing costs in every financial roll-up is no joy, either. Down deep, Pete feels his handpicked people are failing him. Since taking over as CEO five years ago, Pete knows he has worked hard, attracting eagles from the competition and promoting rising stars from within. He's focused on putting the right people in the right slots.

His president and chief operations officer, Jim, came up through the ranks, starting in sales, with intermediate stops in running manufacturing operations, handling the Far East, and stewardship of the Strategic Products Group.

Together, Pete and Jim have carefully selected a real pro from their leading competitor to head up all manufacturing operations. They cherry-picked one of IBM's best to run corporate MIS, and the new head of research and development is not only young and energetic, but also the most brilliant individual Pete has ever worked with. His management team should be a dream team. Still, it is clear to Pete (and to a few key Board members) that the company isn't being priced accordingly by the Wall Street crowd.

Pete pushes away from his desk and walks over to the window. A few wisps of smoke can be seen curling from the stacks of the company's original facility, two miles away. All around it are homes, schools, and businesses of their home city.

Pete knows he employs over a quarter of the workers in town. His payroll bankrolls this community and a dozen others across the United States, two in Canada, and a number of smaller facilities in Mexico, Germany, and Ireland. Thousands of shareholders, vendors, and employees are depending on him to get the blasted products out the door, on time, and in good enough condition that the marketplace will respond favorably.

At moments like these, Pete asks himself why he didn't choose a career with lower stress, and greater chances for success. Like social work. Or cancer surgery.

Manufacturing malaise has become almost a medical condition for him. He lives with it, sleeps with it, dreams about it, even takes it on vacation with the family. He can be at a charity fundraiser, or at his daughter's seventh grade school play. He can see his reflection before him in the bathroom mirror, lathered and ready to shave. But the image of the giant research and development and manufacturing machine slowing to a halt, and the challenge of getting products from blueprint to rail car in a reasonable amount of time are never far from his thoughts.

There are moments when Pete wonders if he ever really understood manufacturing. But so what — who does? He paid top dollar to bring in the best manufacturing pros. They should surely understand it.

Pete is also mad as hell at the sales force for not selling what they must sell. Pete, like his role model John Akers at IBM, is ticked because his sales reps and their managers are too damned comfortable, too understanding, when they lose to the competition.

At the same time, Pete knows his biggest problem isn't sales — it's new product constipation. The company simply needs to get more new products out faster, that cost less, that incorporate technology and functionality that grab customers' attention.

The ideal? Research and development and manufacturing operations working as a close-knit team, able to turn on a dime. The reality? They are like mammoths mired in tar. Research and development says you *can't create* on a schedule. Manufacturing tells you that without good forecasts their work is impossible and that they are already performing miracles to keep up with constantly changing sales forecasts.

Pete isn't sure anyone has a real handle on cost, either, because way too much is allocated based on direct labor-hours. And labor is now under 20 percent of his product cost. Starting up new lines and shutting down unprofitable ones is a glacier strategy. Pete is now at the point where he just decrees, "Do it," and that doesn't seem to work, either.

It's a pity. Pete loves being a CEO; he enjoys the power and loves the pace. He yearns to beat the pants off the competition. It burns inside him like one of those underground peat fires that never go out. But even though he's working his tail off, as well as the tails of his direct reports, he's still losing ground to faster moving international competitors and to lean competitors on the West Coast and in the Southeast.

He commissioned an expensive study to see how he's doing against competitors in each of his main product lines. The conclusion? His production costs are higher than those of smaller U.S. competitors, and his quality is losing ground to international competitors.

What else can he try? He's pushed the total quality management button, and the just-in-time button, and held them down as long and as hard as anyone. And some things did improve — not the faster cycle time-to-market that he wanted, but productivity increased, rework lessened, inventory controls became more efficient, and customer service received more attention.

But what did it all amount to? The competition was getting better at the same time, and he's not sure if his improvements were in the areas that most needed improving. It's tough to measure performance in any intelligent way across an entire company. All he feels he can do is hold up his hand when asked about quality and improved productivity and say, "Me, too."

Decentralization? Tried it. Split the pie into 10 good-sized product lines, called each one a "company," and made the vice presidents group VPs. It was a big deal in the trade magazines. Big deal, is right — nothing happened.

Cut costs? Please, don't get him started on costs. Sales are up, but so what, when costs are up even more. You try to force them down but it's like sitting on a waterbed — it goes down here, it goes up over there.

Partnering? Lots of companies seem to have been cutting costs by farming out corporate functions to outside vendors.

His company hires outside temps now instead of maintaining a central secretarial pool. Plans are under way to do the same with copying, janitorial, and messenger services. But these costs only scratch the surface. His real expenses are occurring in production. So why not farm out production of some components and shut down some of the less efficient plants? Maybe he could put out bids to some of those hot new contract manufacturers he's been hearing about. Let them do the manufacturing on a cost-plus basis. But should he outsource such a critical function? *If a manufacturer delegates manufacturing, is the manufacturer still a manufacturer?*

His reveries end abruptly when the phone rings. It's the vice president of MIS. She's promising that the latest bolt-on to the company's mainframe MRP II system will once and for all put an end to the complaints they're getting. Right, Pete says to himself. MIS is always calling him. The latest gimmick is always supposed to speed everything up. It never does.

He hangs up, sighs, exhales, and reaches for a cigarette, then remembers he doesn't smoke. It's going to be another long quarter.

THE DOWNTURN OF AMERICAN MANUFACTURING

Pete Bates doesn't exist but he is a realistic composite. Like Pete, I admire and appreciate what manufacturing has done for this country, and I'm worried about what will happen if manufacturing continues its slide.

Since I was a little kid, I've always thought manufacturing was special. Turning raw materials into finished products was so *American*. I know, we didn't invent manufacturing, but we were the best at it. I remember seeing what the lively spirit of manufacturing could do for a country, just after World War II and in the glory decades that followed.

I grew up in the boot heel of Missouri, the "Show-Me State." My dad ran a factory that made all kinds of caps and hats for J C Penney. As a kid, I saw a factory as Americans of every stripe, background, and accent, working side by side in a big, long building, with windows of Coke-bottle green glass. One end of the building housed water-resistant cloth of every color and fabric, and at the other end all types of hats rolled out one after another: St. Louis Cardinal caps; deerstalker caps, like Sherlock Holmes wore; and strangely shaped camouflage-green gardening hats with nylon mesh hanging down to keep bees and mosquitoes away while you bent over to pick a few tomatoes.

America was full of factories like that. We were like magic croupiers — every time we shuffled a deck of cards straight flushes turned up in the form of merchandise and products the world was lining up to buy.

Mass production and value adding. The magic lay in mass production and value adding. Manufacturing was king, and America was king of manufacturing. There is scarcely a more potent image for the economic might of this country than the picture of Henry Ford's Rouge Plant in Detroit; 24 square miles of assembly lines, kicking out a shiny new car every 17 seconds. It was a vision of the factory as a universe unto itself, a dream of centralized controls brought to life by great design, engineering, and management.

The only problem was, America's manufacturing magic was wearing off, and fast. In the 1960s, we saw our consumer electronics industry fall prey to foreign competition. In the 1970s, it was steel and automobiles. By the 1980s, semiconductors were the victims. Our most cherished industries, suddenly humbled! We not only didn't believe it, we didn't even see it. It was as hard to admit our decline in competitiveness as it is difficult to see our own faces age one day at a time. But no matter how you measure it, American manufacturing today is not producing as well as it ought to, as well as it used to, or as well as our competitors have learned to.

How manufacturing stands today. By my count there are about 350,000 manufacturing enterprises in the United States, that in turn own and run about half a million domestic factory sites. The largest companies have the most factory sites, of course. America's 50 largest individual companies average about 150 manufacturing sites apiece. The 500 largest enterprises, as a group, average 25 sites. And so it goes, until you trip over the many thousands of small one-roof manufacturers.

How well are these 500 companies doing? The press covers every hiccup from a *Fortune* 500 company. We know a lot about them — so much, in fact, that we lose perspective on their actual performance. To be blunt about it, the business press hasn't got a clue what's really happening out there. They just repeat what they are told — it's called reporting. But the world of customers has a pretty good handle on how these companies are doing. They are giving our biggest companies a test even as you read this, and it will not be graded on a curve.

Consider the findings in the June 1992 *World Competitiveness Report*, an international publication that annually tracks how individual national environments have helped or hurt the domestic and global competitiveness of enterprises operating in those countries. The report analyzes the overall competitiveness of 22 industrialized nations (e.g., the United States, Germany, Japan, U.K., etc.) and 14 newly industrialized economies (e.g., Singapore, Taiwan, Mexico, India, etc.).[1]

Let me net out for you what I think this report says to America: overall, we have the strongest, most productive, most resilient economy this planet has ever known. What other country could have created the enormous number of service-sector jobs created here in the past 10 years? A lot of newly industrialized countries would love to trade their problems for ours. On the sobering side, however, for the seventh year in a row Japan has come in number one in overall competitiveness. Japan's strength remains its lead in R&D, management, education, and its powerful domestic economy. The United States has fallen from third to fifth place since 1990, and the report concludes that the United States has further to fall. This Rock of Gibraltar that we've relied upon and enjoyed for so long is showing serious signs of stress and fatigue. The foundation has cracked. Our forefathers mothballed the Liberty Bell after it cracked. (See the table on the following page.)

Also revealing was information in previous editions that zeroed in on "share of world exports," showing long-term trends separately for each industrialized country. Each country's top-10 leading exports, be it coal or cars, were plotted on a line graph in terms of percentage share of world exports over a 20-year period. If the line rose over time, a country was gaining share. If the line dropped, they were losing market share.

These charts offer little comfort. Japan's trend lines rose in virtually all of their top-10 export categories. Germany's trend lines remained level. The U.S. trend lines? Nearly all down.

The truth is, increases in U.S. productivity over the past 20 years have proceeded at a pace of wretched slowness. Our standard of living has been at a standstill over that period while other industrialized countries have made startling

Where We Stand
(numerical ranking among top 22 industrialized nations)

Domestic Economic Strength	**U.S.**	**Japan**	**Germany**
Gross domestic product (GDP)	1	2	3
GDP per capita	9	6	7
Strength of manufacturing base	14	1	4
International Performance			
Balance of trade in services	1	21	12
Balance of merchandise trade	22	2	1
Management Prowess			
Labor productivity	14	12	1
Capital productivity	2	22	7
Manufacturing productivity	11	1	7
Production technologies	14	1	2
Proper use of information technology	7	1	5
Growth in R&D expenditures	18	7	12
Cycle time to market	6	1	8
Price/quality ratio of products	8	1	2
Total quality control	13	1	2
Customer service	7	1	3
Competitiveness of Work Force			
Educated to meet needs of a competitive economy	21	4	2
In-company training	17	1	2
Worker motivation	10	1	4
Computer literacy	14	1	7

Source: *World Competitiveness Report*, June 1992

advances. Real wages on an hourly basis have been headed south since 1973. This from the country that invented time-motion studies, scientific management, the assembly line, and quality control!

American consumers face a real dilemma. Prices have been going up for years, while income has been going nowhere. The average price for a new car in 1990 was just over $16,000. Even adjusted for inflation, that is a lot of money for most people to pay for personal transportation. Paired against the median family income of $32,000, we see that a car costs roughly half what most families make in a year. Not many of us are going to buy a new car every other year at those prices.

What country will rule the economic roost in the 21st century? Only 30 percent of U.S. citizens say it will be the United States; 53 percent say it will be Japan.

What emerges from all these statistics is a picture of the American manufacturing sector slowing to a crawl, bumping against performance measures it can't hope to surpass, doomed by the sheer mass of its greatest companies, and the inflexibility that goes with bulk, slipping to the ranks of a second-rate manufacturer.

The capital crisis. Capital formation is another area in which the United States lags. Capital formation is the money available to a country to do the things it wants to do. Traditionally, America has always been able to finance its growth. In the post–cold war world, other countries are suddenly pushing ahead of us in the line for loans.

Our trade and budget deficits continue to handicap us. And our business practices are likely to make matters worse. Whereas Japanese and European companies rely heavily on debt to finance expansion, we have relied more on equity capital. The problem is that investors are turning to global markets with their money, and U.S. companies are simply not attracting as much of the worldwide equity-capital pie as they need. Moreover, competing countries, because they kept their noses comparatively clean in the paper-chase, takeover, and leveraged buyout economy of the 1980s, are able to borrow at lower rates than we can.

On every capital formation front, we appear to be at a disadvantage. The cost of debt is higher for us than for European and Japanese companies. The sales price of our stocks, our price-to-earnings ratio through the 1980s, was one-fourth of Japan's, meaning Japan has all this extra money to bring to the table. Meanwhile, U.S. corporations pay high taxes, siphoning off chunks of profits that could be recycled into production.

How much in debt are we? The top 1,300 companies in 1992 have a 42 percent ratio of debt to total capitalization and have operating income equal to only 2.2 times their interest payments, compared with 25 percent and 5.2 times, respectively, in 1980.

Whether employing debt or equity, Japanese and European corporations hold a "cost of funds" advantage over U.S. competitors. They have lots of money brought in at attractive rates, a status that appears likely to continue for the near term, while our funds are looking scarcer and scarcer, and costing more and more.

How much more of this can we take? We are like a camel that could carry a lot. America is a country with such abundant human and natural resources that, over the past few decades, we have tended to shrug as our system placed a few extra straws on our back. We were strong; we could handle it.

But over time those straws have accumulated. Increasing labor costs. Adversarial union relationships. Business tax Ping-Pong. The corporate raider phenomenon. Golden parachutes. Political paralysis. Junk financing. The fluctuating dollar. Intra- and inter-company turf wars. Excessive regulations. The collapse of the thrifts. Falling back to centralized controls at a time when American business desperately needs the exact opposite, the empowerment of small, autonomous work teams. The constant deprecation by U.S. industry of its own manufacturing people. And everywhere, on every wavelength, a torrent of talk, talk, talk.

Eventually the camel collapses.

MANUPHOBIA: FEAR OF MANUFACTURING

The truth is that American manufacturing has lost its most precious asset, its confidence. I call it *manuphobia*, the gnawing fear executives have that they don't understand and have lost all control over what happens on the factory floor. American manufacturing is an impostor today, going through the motions of manufacturing excellence, afraid to attempt the real thing. Instead of making things, we have others make them for us. Where we were once the number-one source of ideas, innovation, and a can-do attitude, we now make a common practice of having a subcontractor in a low-wage country do it for us.

Our largest industrial companies are rushing headlong toward manufacturing outsourcing. They are busily shutting down plants, trimming capacity, and slashing overhead. It is as if some supernatural force were telling manufacturers to get out of manufacturing. And they are getting out while the getting is bad.

The illusion of manufacturing. An *Industry Week* interview with Sidney Harman, founder of Harman-Kardon and

Harman International, said it about right: "Too many American companies have simply abandoned the business of being in manufacturing. Instead, they just pretend they are manufacturers. They're content to stick their labels on products others make or have manufacturing assembly shops build products to their specifications."[2]

I agree. That's not manufacturing, that's a Potemkin village, a series of facades made up to look like manufacturing.

The flexible system of in-out manufacturing perfected in such Japanese companies as Toyota and Matsushita could not be more different from the slow, lumbering, unintelligent system practiced at American companies through the 1980s. Where the Japanese could make money building small batches of things, America was wedded to the concept of mass assembly, believing that short runs were inherently unprofitable.

In Japan, they learned to develop the product and the process for manufacturing the product simultaneously. Here we have always had designers dream up the product on one side of the corporate wall, then toss it over to production engineers on the other side — an enjoyable, low-accountability way to earn a living, but no way to manufacture.

In Japan, inventory strove for leanness — no waste. In America, we built automated warehouses so we could be extremely efficient at moving inventory, lots and lots of it — "just in case."

In Japan, vendors were made part of the family. In America, we played vendors one off the other, in the name of economy, with the result being resentment and aloofness.

In Japan, everyone in a company was expected to know and care about one another's responsibilities. In America, we practiced repetitive specialization and compartmentalization. Workers labored in a kind of walled box, unconcerned about their coworkers' duties.

In Japan, quality plus continuous process improvement stood at the center of a work force's pride and a company's strategy. In America, quality was a marketing term — something you said you had even if you didn't. And corporate strategy was geared toward the "windfall product": the Mustang, the Instamatic, the blockbuster product that paid for all others.

In Japan, meeting customer needs was the galvanizing force driving a business. They used the image of a magnet, "pulling" products through to market.

Japan didn't make us into a Potemkin village. We did it to ourselves. We did it when we decided, sometime after World War II, that bottom-line financial managers were more important than on-site plant managers. "Moving the chips around" in a high-stakes game was worth a lot more than manufacturing chips.

Discouragement and decay. David Halberstam, in *The Reckoning*,[3] documented the growing gulf between central finance and local operations at Ford Motor Co. "The managers felt themselves buffeted by the ever more frequent directives from Detroit. That was bad enough. But unlike their predecessors they had to achieve Detroit's requirements in a new unionized age, and it was harder now to turn the screws on workers. So they had learned to deceive Detroit as best they could in order to preserve the integrity of their own operations.

"Were there too many parts left over at the end of a model's life? Headquarters hated that, so each year the plant people faithfully reported that they had only sixty-two of one part and only forty-eight of another. Detroit, they assured the home office, had been every bit as efficient at planning as it hoped. Meanwhile, they simply dumped the excess parts into the nearby Delaware River."

Ford was a massively centralized operation that communicated to its real manufacturing experts, intentionally or not, that their experience and judgment were without value and what mattered was the integrity of central planning.

It's fine that plant managers devised a "gray market" so they could actually go about their business of making cars despite the importunings of the buttoned-down decision makers in Dearborn. Short term, Ford met its production targets, and the whiz-kids were happy. But in the longer term, it was apparent to every worker at Ford's hundreds of manufacturing sites around the world, that they had little respect and no status in the company's big picture. They were merely implementers; when told to do something, they did it. In the great turf war between central management and line manufacturers, line manufacturers had lost, and losing meant being stripped of autonomy. The people most responsible for America's championship status as world-class manufacturers were being reduced to gofers.

Declining status. As one generation retires and the next takes its place, the memory of what made you great gradually fades, and the original requirements for innovation and leadership blur. Eventually you have a multitier system in which central headquarters drives the entire manufacturing engine, though it may know next to nothing about shop-floor manufacturing. This is a system in which plant managers are guys who check their brains at the door when they come to work and skew the numbers to shade the truth.

How many CEOs of *Fortune* 1000 companies do you suppose came up through the production ranks? Fewer than 8 percent, according to a *Fortune* magazine survey.[4] While we give a great deal of lip service to the importance of hands-on manufacturing experience, the truth is that most top executives don't want plant people attending their cocktail parties, much less marrying their daughters or sons.

This view of manufacturing as a second-rate vocation has trickled down through our entire society. A hundred years ago, Horatio Alger wrote an inspired series of short novels about plucky young men who rose from poverty to assume one of society's most prestigious roles, running a factory. But a combination of societal factors — environmental fervor, plant closings, and the systematic decline, at the hands of centralized management, of the prestige of manufacturing — has made manufacturing types suspect in the popular imagination.

Turn on the TV today and you'll hear a tremendous amount of undifferentiated excitement about colas, investment opportunities, clothes, vacation spots, cars, and even TV itself. The world is driven by hype and hysteria. But where is the enthusiasm for the engine that drove us to our current pinnacle of prosperity?

Who speaks for manufacturing? I don't mean some dusty industry council or behind-the-scenes lobbying group or even the cloistered hoopla of the Malcolm Baldrige National Quality Award. What I mean is why don't we see our business and political leaders who are in the public eye hustling our greatest economic treasure with the same excitement with which they hawk their products, election campaigns, or personal ambitions? When it was on top, U.S. manufacturing had many patrons; now that it is struggling and needs help, it is a virtual orphan.

A little test that deserves an honest answer! Do you want your child to graduate from college and aspire to run a big plant? In Japan, parents do.

In earlier times, manufacturing was seen in the United States as a pathway out of poverty and toward progress. Today, smokestacks strike young people as vaguely sinister. Today's youth might see the calling of a forest ranger or oceanographer as far more glorious than a manufacturer's. Manufacturing has fallen into popular disfavor in part because of the relative glamour of Wall Street. Why would a business school *wunderkind* turn to the dirty, long-hours drudgery of plant life when new graduates can make better money quicker in consulting, finance, and other "glamorous" service areas?

Perhaps this attitude is helping to fuel the sale of American manufacturing capacity. Overseas concerns currently control 13 to 15 percent of American industrial assets. Britain is the largest foreign owner of U.S. manufacturing companies today, but look for Japan to take the top spot one day soon.

A recent study from the National Association of Manufacturers spells it out more plainly. Only 59 percent of American engineering graduates go into manufacturing; in Japan that figure is 70 percent. And even those young professionals who do go into manufacturing can find their career advancement blocked by people with nonmanufacturing backgrounds. At Reynolds Metals, only 5 of the company's 25 executive officers came up through the plants, and no chief executive officer ever did.

The partnering chimera. One of the latest manifestations of manuphobia has been the proliferation of "partnering" relationships between large corporations and smaller vendors. IBM, for instance, has contracted with Baldrige Award-winning Solectron to build many of its components. IBM benefits by eliminating a problematic part of its immediate work load; Solectron benefits by establishing a lifelong, blue-chip business alliance. On the face of it, it's a win-win situation.

Partnering agreements exist for just about every product, process, and function. Eastman Kodak has partnering agreements with IBM to handle its mainframe computer services; with Businessland to handle its PC procurements; and with Digital Equipment to handle many of its telecommunications tasks.

Partnering is a logical, intelligent option for a company that acknowledges its own weaknesses and is willing to cut its costs by letting another company take over some part of its business. I am a strong advocate of partnering — letting other companies take over functions they can do better and more cheaply, enabling you to "stick to your knitting." *But when you find yourself "partnering off" the knitting itself, you had better make plans to get out of the sweater business.*

Partnering is a slippery slope for managers. If it works to outsource A, why not outsource B, C, and D? The most startling partnering relationships are those in which companies previously known for their manufacturing throw up their hands and turn key manufacturing functions over to outsiders. IBM's partnership with Solectron has been hailed as a brave step. But what will IBM's next step be? Will Solectron take over several of IBM's existing manufacturing facilities?

This kind of partnering is celebrated in the press as a visionary or clever move. But it troubles me, because in the process the company may go too far by subcontracting business functions that are critical to its identity. What is a software development company that sells software, but farms out actual software coding? What is a steel company that no longer makes its own steel? What is a car company that enters into a strategic agreement to have its competitor make cars bearing its nameplate?

Partnering at this extreme is a sign of the worst kind of manuphobia — it is a white flag. The company is confessing to the world that it is not what it once was and has given up competing in its most central, mission-critical function — making things. It erodes the company's reason for being in business.

Companies, after all, have only three essential tasks: to create, make, and market products or services for customers. Companies have been partnering off marketing functions to dealers, distributors, ad agencies, PR firms, and research groups for years. Many companies have taken the additional step of buying other companies to short-circuit the process of product development. But the worst abdication of corporate responsibility has to be declaring that a manufacturer will no longer make its own products.

The point is not that companies should build walls around themselves and not outsource corporate tasks. Instead, a new concept of the corporation-vendor relationship is gaining ground. It sees parent companies as mentors to their suppliers. IBM maintains an on-site presence at the Solectron factory, for example, working to ensure conformance to quality standards. Many world-class companies, such as Motorola and Xerox, insist that their vendors conduct Baldrige Award self-assessments if they are to continue as corporate partners.

These are good practices. What is not good is the corrosion of the manufacturing company's prime function. You partner off your tasks one at a time, then one day you realize you've partnered away everything of substance. When that happens, you are no longer a manufacturing company. You are not much of anything. You are, however, what the Japanese mock — the lazy or fearful American company that has given up on what it used to do best, and taken up shuffling paper instead. You are just a deal maker, clutching a handful of chits.

THE CEO'S DILEMMA

Manufacturing has fallen so far that most people simply have given up on it as an important part of American's future. John Naisbitt's contributions to contemporary crystal-balling (he predicts the future by counting newspaper clippings) have centered on the inevitable decline of dirty, smelly, noisy manufacturing, which we will subcontract to the less-developed nations that don't mind a little dirt, smell, and noise, and on the refashioning of the American economy as largely service-driven.

Much is made of our reformulation into a service economy. The service sector currently provides 70 percent of jobs, with manufacturing picking up the slack — down about 15 percent from a generation ago. And that statistic is likely to accelerate, no matter what manufacturing does. Automation and outsourcing will prevent manufacturing from boosting its numbers, and the so-called service sector will continue to grow.

But it's an apples-to-oranges debate. Take McDonald's. With over 10,000 locations worldwide and continuing rapid expansion, this "services" company alone affects the numbers. But McDonald's, with its sophisticated JIT inventory schemes and advanced production technologies, has a foot in both the service and manufacturing sectors and closely resembles a demassified multisite, low-end assembly manufacturer. One reason why some American service companies are on the upswing is precisely that they are defining themselves in terms originated by manufacturing.

Consider the alternative: could McDonald's maintain its remarkable rate of growth if it simply designed great food products, and then licensed its production and marketing to third parties? Could it outsource production and sell what others cook and assemble for them to private label?

The conventional answer is of course not. Profitability increases when you control the means of production. However, Pepsico's Taco Bell is challenging conventional wisdom by farming out as much food preparation as possible and reducing kitchen space from 70 percent to 30 percent of a typical outlet.[5]

Bucking the megatrends. I think Taco Bell's outsourcing strategy is short-term, bottom-line helpful — and long-term, bottom-line disastrous. The conventional wisdom still works, and what is true for hamburgers is equally true for manufacturing. Outsource your peripheral functions, those not essential to your company and its mission. But never outsource what differentiates you from your competition, what makes you unique. For then you lose your reason for being in the market, and the market will know it, and your company will surely die.

Product and service have coexisted so long that each has taken on many of the conceptual characteristics of the other. Richard Schonberger's "chain of customers" concept redefines service as the extent to which every team within a manufacturing company serves every other team.[6] According to this theory, good service can be abstract or concrete, depending on the individual work team's business. It can be doing a good job at accounting, flipping hamburgers, handling customer complaints, or warehousing steel pipe (for purposes of examination, all are comparable).

So when you hear the service/product debate start up, listen closely. The lines between the two worlds have become so blurred, and the management approaches so similar, that the former distinctions have lost much of their meaning.

What managers can do. CEOs often find themselves on the receiving end of criticism because so much — our prosperity, our way of life, our children's futures — depends on the choices they make. In truth, today's typical CEO of a manufacturing company, like Pete Bates, has responsibilities perhaps too heavy for one person to bear.

While most CEOs have never personally run a manufacturing operation, they must still understand how one works, where its strengths and bottlenecks are, what works and what doesn't. Besides understanding that past failures should not be repeated, CEOs must also recognize which new opportunities to pursue, as promising production-process innovations surface.

The two conventional alternatives laid out for most CEOs are simple enough, and about equally exciting. Stay centralized, or try decentralizing. There is a third alternative, of course, and that is the subject of this book. But for the moment, let's look at the first two choices.

Stay centralized. As CEO, you may retain controls at the top, in a highly centralized configuration, thus holding onto the maximum amount of prerogatives. You're the boss, and everyone reports to you. Succeed, and you will soar. Fail (and individuals are often no match for a bureaucracy of 100,000 or so employees), and chances are that no one — stockholders, directors, customers, or employees — will remember your name when you're gone.

Decentralize. Yes, you may keep control centralized, or you may restructure your company into stand-alone divisions, which is classic decentralization. You share responsibilities with the heads of your main business divisions. You keep a lean yet effective headquarters team to track results and offer advice. You can boast that decentralization has created a profound sense of intracorporate entrepreneurship and pride, when all you have really done is add another layer of management.

The problem with conventional decentralization schemes, like the one announced by IBM in early 1992, is that they normally divide one large mass into several smaller, but still oversized, masses. You have not made your company more manageable, you've simply spread your risk to a number of subordinate managers who are, by definition, less competent than you.

Meanwhile, no matter which route you take, the various divisions and departments within your company progressively lose sight of the real enemy — the competition. Why wouldn't they? They haven't seen real faces or crossed swords in years!

Turf wars break out between purchasing and accounting; between design and engineering; between production and finance. Manufacturing is at information services' throat, and vice versa. Bomb after bomb is lobbed over divisional walls.

Too many big businesses today are run by executives who navigate while peering into their company's rear-view mirror. At the heart of the six-digit-employee company, or the five-digit division sits an expensive mainframe computer crammed with last year's numbers, last year's priorities, and last year's critical action messages. Its speed and comprehension are unquestioned, but its ability to communicate is mysteriously absent.

While you and your trusted associates labor to put out yesterday's fires, today's problems are hitting your company like a pile-driver. Costs are rising faster than you can raise prices. Company warehouses are sagging from the weight of just-in-case inventories. New product cycle time-to-market keeps stretching out. Research and development people are tearing their hair out, and plant managers are beating their dogs.

Over 75 percent of your centralized software staff resources are tied up in systems maintenance resulting in long queues for needed new systems. Even public relations is morose, and they're not allowed to be.

The people in accounting look at the floor when you walk by; you sense that major new write-offs are lurking under that rug they keep looking at. And you haven't the foggiest idea whether the numbers that plop on your desk by the 10th of the month bear any resemblance to reality. At best they reflect how the company did last month, but they don't help much in focusing on what's going wrong now or what will go wrong tomorrow. And the Board asks, "What's going to happen next month?" You wish there were someone you could ask and expect a reasonably informed answer.

Meanwhile, somewhere across an ocean, the competition is serenely going about the task of bludgeoning your market share, point by point. God knows how, but somehow they seem to know what they are doing.

2
How We Got Into This Mess

We got into this mess because of a little bit of arrogance, and a whole lot of breakdown in communications as successful companies became massive. Authority became centralized because it gave those at the top a greater feeling of control. Also, large computers had been effectively promoted as the absolutely necessary way to collect, crunch, and synthesize data. But centralized control turned out to be a contradiction in terms.

If there was ever a single overriding issue for a company, it's Who's in charge here? There are all sorts of legitimate answers to that question. I'm in charge. You're in charge. We're in charge. Somebody must be in charge, right?

Most observers agree that there are two broad types of organizational structures, whether in government or business: centralized and decentralized. They are easy to distinguish. Centralized means top-down organization, with power held firmly at the top of the pyramid. This type of organization occurs when the person at the top is strong and a high percentage of subordinates need direction, or are perceived to need direction.

Decentralized means that substantial amounts of corporate power have been distributed to key points within the organization. This type of organization emerges when a high percentage of the company's top managers are strong, or perceive themselves to be strong. This also occurs when a company gets in deep trouble and the CEO finds organizational change preferable to a mandatory career change.

Whether a company follows a centralized or decentralized course, control is always the critical issue. Neither centralized nor decentralized control is intrinsically good or bad. Companies can be run well or poorly with either structure. Neither structure is incompatible with or exclusive of the other.

Many companies have both centralized and decentralized features. The best way to think of them is as points on a continuum.

THE THEORY OF CENTRALIZATION

Which is best when? Obviously, in a one-person company, centralization is the only way to go. It is also attractive for a company with a narrow product line, or for a company with a single geographical location, a company producing commodity products or services, or a company that may have many employees but few functional distinctions. If your only business is coal mining, it might be foolish to decentralize. If your company does only a single block function, such as making aluminum, running a hotel, growing bananas, or burning coal to create electrical power, nothing may be achieved by decentralizing.

Centralization is undoubtedly the most expeditious way to run a company in its early stages, until growth takes it to such a level that a lone individual has trouble keeping the company on course.

Move too early toward some kind of decentralized system, and you make management more complicated than it needs to be. Delay moving to decentralization too long and your company may topple from its own unsupported weight.

Concepts of centralization turn on the idea of distance — between locations, between levels or operations, and between the level of decision making and decision enactment. *Centralized* organization works best when distance is modest or when the problems caused by distance are inconsequential. *Decentralized* control works best when distance is significant and is clearly a problem, and greater local control appears warranted.[1]

The heart of centralization is maintaining prerogatives of top management. If you are a do-everything-yourself executive, a top-down control kind of leader, centralization is for you. What are its promises? Focused strategy, more efficient use of capacity, more specialized staffs, tighter control of costs, and tighter security and control over sensitive information. In general, fewer loose ends.

Centralization reportedly makes the most sense in terms of tight cost controls. Until the late 1970s, nearly everyone writing on the subject stated unequivocally that, regardless of its other impacts, centralization controlled expenditures best, thus saving money and increasing profitability. When you get only one phone bill, you know if you are paying too much. Buying gasoline by the shipload is cheaper than buying it at the pump. In addition, central computing certainly beats buying redundant computing equipment for every division.

Managers who opt for a centralized structure are often very good managers. A major attraction of centralization is that the CEO can know more about how everything in the company works than anyone else. (Knowing less than 100 percent of what's going on is, after all, a horror for any red-blooded CEO.) Centralization is a sensible policy until a company grows to a certain size, then the savings of power consolidation are offset by the unwieldiness of sheer mass.

The trouble with centralization. CEOs are kidding themselves, of course, if they imagine they have extensive expertise in every business discipline. In lieu of actual experience and knowledge, prejudices about these disciplines arise. Here are a few examples of misguided wisdom:

Misguided Wisdom on Centralization

Management: "Make economies of scale work for us. We've got the critical mass — let's leverage the stuffing out of it."
"Leave important strategic decisions to the professionals. Lower-level employees are paid to execute, period."

Engineering: "Keep design engineers away from manufacturing. They'll argue more than they'll collaborate."
"Keep 'em apart. 'Group gropes' by people with different biases and temperaments lead to marathon meetings, endless problem solving, interminable woolgathering, all of which lead to 'late to market.'"

Line Foremen: "Keep work lined up for your people to do. Keeping people busy and machines running full blast makes everyone look good. That's what productivity is all about."

Purchasing: "Buying in large lots gives us leverage on the deal."
"Be careful that you don't rely too much on a few vendors. Let them know you have lots of other options. Keep them on their toes and competitive. Go to 'How to Negotiate' seminars and learn how to systematically squeeze the hell out of them."

Accounting: "Labor content is the only reliable criterion for allocating costs. It may not be perfect, but it's a lot better than whatever is second best. And, if you people at the top expect accurate reporting, make sure everyone keeps feeding in those numbers to us here on the 14th floor."

Information Services: "Large companies need large computers with all the corporation's data assets under the tight control of experts who know what they're doing. Standards are what is important. Keeping all interfaces and corporate data elements in sync is necessary to prevent anarchy. Let those undisciplined departments loose to do their own things, and they'll create a mess no one can clean up."

I am a collector of oxymorons: contradictions in terms such as jumbo shrimp, live recording, athletic scholarship, and guest host. *Centralized control* is an oxymoron. If you are at the center of something gigantic, you are not likely controlling it.

You could dig a hole to the center of the earth, and set up shop there, but you would not be in control of the planet. You would in fact be the blindest person in the world.

To have 20/20 vision of an entire landscape, one must be outside it. A single perspective will not do; you need many sets of eyes. As with a televised football game, you need many camera angles and lenses — slow-motion, reverse angle, upfield, downfield, long shot, close-up — to pick up all the action.

Centralization's primary appeal is probably that it makes the central figure, the CEO, *feel* like a central figure, the hands-on commander on whom all corporate life depends. Centralization is inherently enamored with "global thinking," that is, brilliant on the broad issues, but too busy to focus on the details beneath the surface.

Big problems call for big technological solutions. Image problem? Big ad campaign. Profits problem? Call in McKinsey. Data problem? Bigger mainframe. Huge, infallible, and invincible, mass overpowers all that stands in its path. Size is a beguiling conceit; it has attracted the most talented and ambitious individuals and brought about the downfall of many of them. For in truth, to be a successful centralist one must be an extraordinary individual. I'm not talking about *ordinary* extraordinary individuals; we all know a few of those. I'm talking about one in a million.

One of the funniest "Saturday Night Live" skits involved Dan Aykroyd as Jimmy Carter, manning a 24-hour emergency telephone counseling service. One by one the calls came in. One caller was having problems with his car's transmission. Another wondered what the meaning of life was. Yet a third had just taken some pills and didn't know what they were. One by one, Carter, a committed manager but an ineffective leader who was unable to delegate minor matters, attempted to solve each problem himself, right down to explaining to the third caller what each pill's generic name was, its proper use, and what its side effects were.

The Achilles' heel of centralization is that it overloads the people at the top of the company. As centralization waxes, the ability to delegate and trust those lower on the totem pole inevitably wanes. Eventually Napoleon found he extended himself beyond his ability to maneuver (Waterloo), and Caesar was put upon by neglected subordinates (Brutus).

Historian Paul Kennedy believes that one reason the Western (European and American) tradition was more vigorous over the centuries than the richer East was that Europe had always been a cluster of decentralized nation-states. Its rivers, mountains, and natural borders prevented the buildup of vast empires, as occurred in the endless reaches of central Asia. This continuing focus on the local was the cause of much dissension over the years, but out of the competition came the progress that made the Western nations the world's industrial leaders.[2]

Centralization and the Soviet Union. The Soviet Union is a vivid example of the results of overcentralization. From the earliest days of the USSR, centralization was the only option. A new government, surrounded by enemies within and outside the country's borders, had no option except to concentrate what power it could amass in the hands of central authority, the Communist Party.

The problem was that centralization never peaked. It just continued to grow for 70 years. Farms were collectivized, all property was nationalized, and all economic planning was conducted in Moscow, regardless of fluctuations in supply and demand at the thousands of points of commerce scattered across that vast land.

The stories of waste and misdirection by the centrally controlled economy are legion. A steam-generating plant, assigned an annual productivity quota, achieved it by creating volumes of steam heat in midsummer, when demand for heat is slack. A bedframe factory, told to produce 10 tons of bedframes annually, met its goal by manufacturing frames out of iron instead of wood.

The phrase *market-driven* had no meaning in the Soviet Union. In a centrally controlled economy, the driving force is not consumer demand, efficiency, or on-the-spot observation; the state dictates its plan from afar, and local economies work to comply with that plan. Irrational pricing, overcentralized management, and an obsolete industrial infrastructure led to a meltdown of the Soviet Union, first as a superpower, and eventually as an entity of any kind. In the government's last months, lines in Soviet stores were endless and product offerings meager, despite Mikhail Gorbachev's attempted reforms.

While Gorbachev will undoubtedly be hailed by historians as the spark plug for a brave new era, his halting step in the direction of freedom, "market socialism," was doomed by its own internal contradictions. Soviet-style socialism was predicated on central controls. The ultimate breakup into independent states was a necessary and logical step for a massive nation that was choking on its own complexities. Clearly, the new Commonwealth of Independent States has many miles to go in rehabilitating economies hampered by generations of central control.

Lifestyles of the rich and humongous. In the United States, centralized companies have historically developed around the talents of a single individual, the company founder, by definition an entrepreneurial type. Or they form around the person who succeeds after the founder, a driver who grabs the reins to prevent the runaway company from riding off the cliff, but in so doing commits the company to a course so tightly controlled that, over time, it runs into a new set of perils: stagnation, inflexibility, and the rasping sound of the wheels of a mighty institution grinding to a halt.

There are lots of examples of both types of centralizers. In Detroit, for instance, two of the "Great Centralizers," Henry Ford and Henry Ford II, went head-to-head against decentralized General Motors. Henry Ford was the entrepreneur who refused to relinquish control; Henry Ford II, the managers' man, overhauled and saved Ford Motor Co., only to turn it over to a new generation of finance-driven centralists.

The elder Ford was remarkable: doctrinaire, indifferent to his market and isolated from useful feedback, a genius in a vacuum. So unappealing were his public statements on the subject of consumer wants ("They can have any color car they want, so long as it's black."), that by 1933 *Fortune* magazine called Ford "the world's worst salesman."

No American corporation was ever run so poorly for so long. Ironically, Ford's mass may have been its greatest asset during hard years. At the beginning of 1946, the company was losing $10 million a month. It was so big that it would have taken another 40 years to whittle it to nothing. Smaller companies, if run as capriciously and in so centralized a fashion, would go belly up in short order.

Henry Ford was a centralist par excellence, so intent on retaining central authority that he regularly performed wholesale purges of central management not so that power could trickle down to their respective business units, but so that he could continue to wield unquestioned authority himself.

A typical example of Ford's business practices is the story of Arjay Miller, who was sent to check on billings at Ford's central HQ in Detroit, and found that instead of the expected corporate payables office with set routines and methodologies, the company's vast payout system was being managed by a band of wizened men wearing green eyeshades. They sat in a room surrounded by huge stacks of bills, some of them several feet high. To Miller's amazement, the bookkeepers were estimating how many millions of dollars there were per foot of stacked invoices. That was their "system."[3]

The Goliath Syndrome. What struck me about the 1990 Exxon Valdez tragedy in Prince William Sound was the requirements for steering that supertanker. A quarter of a mile in length, the ship required four miles to come about. Its great adversary when maneuvering was itself, its own size. It cost a fortune to get it moving, and it cost a fortune to bring it to a stop.

That's the problem with large centralized corporations as well. For very large companies, it's nearly impossible to get the right product out the door in time to compete with smaller, more flexible companies.

Great size, massiveness, critical mass, the Goliath Syndrome — it goes by many names. Not long ago it was thought to be the most desirable of all business attributes. To be big enough to matter, to demand and get the price you want, to cause your competition to react to you — this is the dream of massiveness.

But it is a pipe dream. Massiveness causes far more problems than it solves. It makes a mess of communications. For manufacturing companies, it inhibits speed and flexibility. Far from being a cost container, it has been proven again and again to be a money-eater. It tends to reward those who adopt safe approaches, while discarding those who use their intuition and try to rock the boat, who challenge the way things have always been done, who want to move fast because experience and their gut tells them that waiting means losing market share. Studies conducted in the early 1980s dispelled at least part of the myth of "economies of scale." In the area of research and development, it was shown that smaller firms were getting 24 times the value for their research dollar than the larger and most centralized firms.

Massiveness resists true employee empowerment and blurs whatever sense of identification or ownership workers have over their own projects. Given the choice between control of the processes of production and enlisting team commitment to success, it chooses control every time.

Massiveness builds in incentives for all kinds of corporate sins: procrastination, overstudying, turf wars, and secretiveness. It dulls the appetite for quality by sapping employee pride and individual ownership of products and processes, and it distracts a company from its pursuit of profitability. And while it may challenge its CEOs and top managers to be the best they can be, the fact is that, little by little, sheer massiveness progressively makes a company more unmanageable.

There was once a time when mass in and of itself was convincing, a promise of success. Americans cheered at their own essays in size: the Empire State Building, Hoover Dam, the atomic bomb. But the romance has died. Today, we look about and see the giants struggling — IBM, Chrysler, Citicorp, Sears — and size has become a warning signal that something is wrong.

Massiveness blurs problem ownership; it lengthens cycle time to market, it hurts quality, and it lowers profits. Yet, in the last decade of the millennium we see a trend back to massiveness. The reason, I suspect, has to do with the determination many CEOs have to get their oversized corporations to work one way or another.

Paleontological records are clear on this point: the last dinosaurs were the very biggest.

Reasons for recentralization. There are four excuses companies have for not radically decentralizing,[4] and each is inadequate. The first is a misguided quest for quality. There are still many CEOs who believe that quality can be dictated from the top down. It must be very frustrating when they learn what so many CEOs have had to learn the hard way — that quality requires collaboration and that autocratic best intentions are of secondary importance in the struggle for quality improvement.

CEOs can be the "doctors" of quality, doing everything they can to diagnose problems and prescribe remedies. But the cure itself occurs within the patient, at the level of discrete operations—the second that can be shaved off an operation here, the waste of a quarter of a gram of metal there, the prevention of a moment of rework farther down the line. Only the people who work at that level can make things better. The task of a CEO is to give workers the responsibility and the tools to do the job.

The second force behind the recent wave of recentralization was Wall Street's instability. Throughout the 1980s takeover mania distracted the best of us from "tending to our knitting." Companies concerned about falling victim to corporate piracy consolidated power at the penthouse level. And companies that were forced to merge with others saw their numbers blended with their new siblings' numbers, with operational power soaring straight to the top of the new parent corporation. At the very moment when companies needed to become more competitive by empowering employees at all levels, companies did the exact opposite to fend off unwanted buyout advances.

Third, the specter of a "United States of Europe" has confused many American companies into thinking that only sheer massiveness on our side can stand up to a fortified Super Europe. But the European Community will probably improve itself more through greater flexibility, fewer trade barriers, monetary union, and reduced language problems than from any foreseeable corporate "massification." Careful observers of the European scene forecast the opposite — a tremendous freeing up of small entrepreneurial companies, the sort of thing we used to be good at.

And the fourth excuse for inching back toward recentralization is plain old ego. Decentralization or demassification *might* improve a company's bottom line, but each requires the sharing of power with a lot of frontline people. There are managers who are their companies' worst enemies, confusing personal "love to command" with what's best for the people they lead and the shareholders they serve.

There are not as many of these "dark angels of industry" as popular myth would have us believe. But we all know managers who fit this description — headstrong individuals who talk and talk, but never listen. In their rush to do what they think is best, they seldom succeed.

THE THEORY OF DECENTRALIZATION

The history of decentralization starts and, in a way, ends with General Motors. Super-powerhouse General Motors, which would one day grow to have over 400,000 salaried workers, 30,000 suppliers, and 10,000 dealers worldwide, did not invent the idea of breaking down large companies into manageable units or divisions. Pierre DuPont was doing much the same thing with his chemical firm for several years before Alfred P. Sloan stumbled upon the principles that drove General Motors toward a remarkable new level of productivity.

DuPont later took his ideas to General Motors, which he headed in the late 1920s, and hired Alfred P. Sloan to manage operations. It was Sloan who formulated an industrial philosophy of decentralization and made it a cause.

"Good management," Sloan said, "rests on decentralization with coordinated control. From coordination we get efficiencies and economies. From decentralization we get initiative, responsibility, development of personnel, decisions close to the facts — all the qualities necessary for an organization to adapt to new conditions."

Decentralization into divisions was Sloan's idea, but it was not created in a dream. Decentralization was a natural for General Motors because that was how it was created — as a family of dissimilar name brands. General Motors had so many obviously discrete businesses that its only option was a decentralized approach.

General Motors began as a hodgepodge of about 30 acquisitions made by General Motors founder Billy Durant. (At one point, Durant came close to adding a fledgling Ford Motor Co. to his stable.) Sloan was manager of one of Durant's 30-odd companies. Eventually, Durant was forced out of GM. (He spent the rest of his life managing a bowling alley.) Alfred Sloan took the helm of the company, as president, CEO, then chairman, from 1923 to 1956.

Sloan was a numbers man, attentive to detail and cost-conscious, but he was much more than that. He was a man of immense concentration. People called him "Silent Sloan" because he seemed to walk in a cocoon, entirely absorbed in dealing with General Motors' production challenges. Out of that cocoon sprang numerous innovations: selling on the installment plan, new car models every year, and increased profits from options and add-ons. But that was nothing compared to the vision he articulated of a company organization — balancing decentralized and autonomous administration and operations against strongly centralized policy making and financial oversight.

The concept was elegant. In theory, people in the divisions would be encouraged to come up with policy ideas and take full responsibility for production, while a few people at the hub of the corporate federation would control the cash.

Decentralization, according to Sloan, worked on three separate planes. It meant decentralization of *power* — a genuine sharing of power from top to bottom; decentralization of *location* — the willingness to let business units locate in the most beneficial places; and decentralization of *function* — moving from central accounting or central computing to accounting and computing at the divisional level.

That the system worked is obvious, by looking at the achievements of General Motors over the span of Sloan's tenure. It was, quite probably, the most successful near half-century experience of any organization in history, success so strong that it lifted and transformed the entire country.

And decentralization is still with us, though its vigor has faded considerably at General Motors and elsewhere. Hardly a year goes by that a major manufacturing company doesn't commit or recommit to the process essentially outlined 70 years ago by Alfred Sloan. In Sloan's day the champions of decentralization were hidebound industrial corporations like General Motors and DuPont. In days to come, there would be new champions, mostly technology companies like Hewlett-Packard, General Electric, Eastman Kodak, and IBM.

Decentralization (the media usually call it "restructuring") is the first resort of companies in pain. It is the aspirin companies take when what is needed is a much more powerful medicine. Unfortunately, the first resort is usually not the best or right resort.

Finding a balance. For many years, companies resisted Sloan's principles of decentralization, feeling that decentralization inherently implies out-of-control, weakened top management. But Peter Drucker argued that decentralization actually strengthens top management: "It makes it more effective and more capable of doing its own tasks."[5]

That, in fact, had been one of the primary lessons of the Japanese experience, and of the pioneering work in organization theory done at IBM. Involving the worker in the problem/solution process actually strengthens management's authority, Drucker said. "It makes management more effective by enabling it to focus on those tasks management needs to perform, and to relieve itself of those tasks which management need not perform, does poorly, and spends far too much time on if loaded down with them."[6]

Decentralization is usually seen as the antidote for too much centralization. When a company gets too hot and heavy at the core, it's time to take some of that heat and move it around to the various company divisions.

Decentralizers tend to focus less on cost reduction and more on increased efficiency and increased customer accessibility. In management information services, for instance, centralization conjures up the image of the mainframe priesthood, a sacred elite who alone understand the secret doings of the company and the machines that, basically, run the company. Decentralization tries to at least break up the priesthood into smaller conclaves—perhaps dropping down from mainframe to minimainframe. At the bottom, no one still has any idea what the computers do, and no one dares ask the computer for data that would actually be useful. But at least, with decentralization, they know what building the computers are in.

The Reagan administration was lauded in its early days for its commitment to decentralized management — the delegation of operating authority to a lower tier of managers (his cabinet) — and the president's celebrated aversion to "micromanagement." *Fortune* magazine ran a special issue headlined, "What Managers Can Learn from Ronald Reagan," which contained insights along the lines of: "Surround yourself with the best people you can find, delegate authority, and don't interfere as long as the policy you've decided on is being carried out."

It is easy to misunderstand the two concepts of centralization and decentralization. Companies don't, as a rule, sit down and vote to centralize or decentralize operations 100 percent. Every company needs a blend of centralization and decentralization, zigging and zagging as situations require. Control is a swinging pendulum, driven by growth, escalating costs, and management trends. And the concept of business as a living, dynamic organism prevents the pendulum from coming to rest.

But now, with U.S. manufacturing in dire need of greater flexibility, savings, and improved total cycle times, the pendulum swings in the direction of decentralization — extreme, even radical decentralization — with real power flowing to local, autonomous business units: what I call demassification.

3
Demassification

Demassification is radical, grass-roots decentralization, with maximum autonomy delegated down to the small, independent business-unit level, and the attendant downsizing of information-processing technology. Although this transformation can be painful, it enriches companies' bottom lines by empowering workers to act independently.

Throughout history, big has meant better. With the arrival of corporate decentralization, that concept had to be qualified: big is better, but breaking big into smaller bits works better. Corporate managers grudgingly concede that there are advantages to smaller size, such as flexibility, speed, and communications. Decentralization, then, is the final word on corporate organization, right?

Wrong! Divisionalized decentralization is a step in the right direction, but it doesn't go far enough; it doesn't demassify. Thus decentralization tends to bump into the same barriers faced by centralized corporations. Before we can understand the difference between demass and decentralization, we need to understand the limits of decentralization.

For most companies, decentralization is viewed as only a trial, not as a restructuring to be implemented in a committed, no-retreat fashion. Management challenges divisions and subdivisions to measure up, gives them a quarter or two to produce results, provides them zero new tools with which to accomplish this, and then yanks the chains back into place at the first sign of distress.

If management does not give its divisions and subdivisions real power, in good faith, then the effort to decentralize is a sham. Companies may announce endless restructurings and still not change what needs to be changed. As long as power rests among a handful of executive officers at the top of an organization, reorganization means little. If decentralization does not follow through by transmitting the tools, the autonomy, and the necessary information, accessible to everyone, it is a waste to attempt it in the first place.

DEFINING DEMASSIFICATION

Demassification is *not* simple, ordinary decentralization.

Every time a major corporation gets into trouble because of eroding market share and profits, management starts talking about restructuring and delegating more autonomy to divisions. This is classical decentralization.

Have you noticed how this restructuring (decentralization) is always described in the press in terms of expected results — "leaner management," "faster decision making," "more market driven" — rather than in terms of what's really being changed in how the business will be run? The unspoken assumption is always that, by delegating more power to five or so senior "subchiefs," the overall company is going to become faster on its feet, pick up market share, and increase profits.

What difference does the addition of five subchiefs make? Is the chief likely to name five subchiefs with viewpoints substantially different from his or her own? Is this new level of management likely to be a breath of fresh air, representing new ideas and new approaches, or just another helping of the "same old same old"?

Classical decentralization may change the way the CEO and president look at the company and at how they may hold responsible a few select executives. But it doesn't change a company's nature, its essential character. Decentralization changes little about the way the company's workers, those closest to the action, do their jobs.

The centralized company that decentralizes down to a few major divisions is basically trying to download and spread the top boss's load among a few trusted lieutenants. Everyone is told this is a big step organizationally, but in reality the division heads alone have been given greater autonomy. That may be great for them, personally, but it doesn't mean squat down below. It's like a captain turning over the quarter deck to his junior officers. The sailors working below deck don't feel a thing.

The lukewarm aggressiveness of decentralization produces exactly the wrong formula for reversing a company's economic decline. It causes upheaval but makes no structural changes. The result is that as decline becomes more evident, it also becomes harder to correct. And management will be able to say, "But — but — but — we decentralized!"

Decentralization should be thought of as "multicentralization" — the establishment of several pockets of primary power instead of one. In contrast, true demassification requires the downflow of actual power and responsibility to the business-unit level, composed of teams of 50, 150, or 250 individuals. Virtually all businesses within a giant corporation can be recast into independent operating units of 250 or fewer people.

DECENTRALIZATION...	DEMASSIFICATION...
is an aspirin	is a cure
is a first step	is a journey
is empowerment to the few	is empowerment to the many
is minimum change to status quo	is a new organizational concept for doing business
doesn't change worker motivation	totally changes worker motivation
can be easily implemented, then de-implemented by a cautious CEO	is tough to implement but even tougher to convince people to go back to the old way
is a breath of fresh air that makes you feel better where you are	is a hurricane that sweeps away the old
is nothing but looking to newly appointed subchieftains and saying, you try and fix it as best you can, as fast as you can	is saying to all workers, "We are going to start operating differently, from stem to stern
is a well-hedged bet, risking little	is a commitment

The meaning of maximum autonomy. What does demassification really change, and what happens when authority and responsibility are distributed to the lowest level? Many large companies have created centralized departments because of their mass of internal customers. These centralized departments are commissioned to provide services cheaper than could be provided by outside companies.

This concept here is terrific. Unfortunately, centralized internal departments don't always stay competitive with outside companies. Over time, they become fat. Consider, for example, central secretarial pools. A central secretarial staff performs secretarial work for any department and usually charges back for its work on a per-page basis. It also provides fill-in secretaries when a regular secretary is absent and charges back on a pay-per-day-of-use basis. Such a department is expected to run on a "zero budget" because it must charge out all its expenses. While most departmental expenses are salaries and employee benefits, there are additional costs for equipment depreciation, space, phone, utilities, training, supplies, stationery, and of course, miscellaneous.

When a corporation with such a central secretarial staff is in trouble, all departmental budgets are squeezed, and internal customers make less use of central secretarial services. Central secretarial services, for its part, can't cut costs without reducing staff. Most large companies don't fire employees in such cases; instead they try to reduce overhead through attrition, accelerated retirement, and so forth. As the central staff tries to maintain a zero budget, it raises its rates. Eventually central staff charges more than outside suppliers.

In a demassified corporation, central secretarial services becomes a small business and the department head is told, "You are to run your department as an independent business. But, if in two years you aren't able to compete on both price and quality of services, then you will be dissolved."

Many kinds of corporate service departments, when challenged, can operate as small independent businesses. To name a few:

- microfilming
- payroll
- food services
- mailroom services

There is no rule that says a demassified corporation cannot retain certain centralized services. If a demassified company chooses to retain centralized functions, however, individuals within them must have dotted-line responsibilities to specific business units.

Let's consider manufacturing, where demassifying means transforming each production unit into a "shop," making the manufacturing corporation a "street of shops." In manufacturing, each department should operate as an independent company and be able to obtain outside customers, if necessary, in order to be "profitable." (The "street of shops" approach at Eastman Kodak is fully described in Chapter 5.) This is not an easy task, since these departments typically have neither sales personnel nor advertising experience. Also, there is a possible conflict if the independent business unit lands a big-bucks contract with an outside customer, but the internal "customer" suddenly decides it wants all the capacity. Operating an internal department as if it were an independent company is difficult and demands more management skill than most internal departments currently are asked to exercise.

A key to operating an internal department as an independent company is for that unit to become so independent that it could move to the outside and actually become a separate business. This is the ultimate level in demassification. Such independence provides corporate management with options it did not have before. One of these new options is to sell the department to the employees, possibly along with a guarantee of a fixed amount of business for a set number of years. Another new management option is to sell the department to another company with which it may have a better strategic fit. The litmus test of a demassified corporation is its ability to successfully divest demassified units without affecting other organizations within the corporation.

Once reorganized into small business units, a corporation must still be managed, but in a different way. A primary role for higher management becomes the setting of guidelines for each demassified unit that spell out how it is to operate and what is expected of it. If a business unit is to operate efficiently for the greater good of the corporation, its tasks must be identified and quantified. Aiming for a more efficient way of doing business does no good if its efficiency is not measurable.

Good, better, best. The conventional corporate wisdom through most of the 20th century has been that centralization is good because it reduces overall expenditures and saves money. In the 1980s, conventional wisdom shifted, now saying that decentralization is better, because it improves efficiency of money expended and gives a company more bang for its buck.

The wisdom of the 21st century and beyond will be that demassification is best because the key to highest return on investment has become speed in decision making and adapting to rapidly changing market environments.

In a little over a quarter of a century, we have gone from survival of the fattest to survival of the fastest. The fastest, clearly, is not a large centralized company. Therefore, the question is not so much *whether* a large corporation should decentralize, but increasingly *how far* to take decentralization and *how rapidly* to proceed.

Demass is decentralization brought down to intimate, hands-on, small-team level. It is the purest form of corporate empowerment.

THE DESIGN OF DEMASSIFICATION

When I am asked what demassification is like, I use as an example the most remarkable practitioner there is, Mother Nature. Think of a beautiful, bountiful, graceful tree, with a trunk of rough brown bark, and a gorgeous canopy of green leaves. Now, though the thought may pain you, think of that tree as a manufacturing enterprise. It is in the business of manufacturing and distributing sap from the raw materials of sunlight, chlorophyll, water, and a few minerals.

If Mother Nature were a centralizer. Mother Nature goes about her work in highly efficient ways. If she were by disposition a centralizer, however, she would have designed a huge trunk, a single root stem, and a single, enormous leaf that would flap above the trunk like a big green circus tent. This gigantic canopy leaf would be the Rouge River Plant of photosynthesis, cranking out sugar to send down the trunk.

That sounds very interesting; in fact, I'd pay to see a tree like that. But nature must not be a centralizer, because to my knowledge, and from what we know of the fossil record, there has never been a tree with one big leaf. It sounds more like a toadstool; it has no nutritive value and could be toxic!

If Mother Nature were a decentralizer. What if Mother Nature were, by nature, into classical decentralization? Then we could go for a walk in the park and admire the beautiful trees that consist of a single trunk, six or eight root stems, and six or eight leaves about the size of large pizzas. Each leaf would be a major production division for the tree. It might make a pretty good poinsettia, but it would be a peculiar tree.

Mother Nature *is* a demassifier. But now we come to the kind of tree we all know and admire — a central trunk carries sap up and nutrients down to an intricate lacework of roots and up to an even more intricate, demassified, interconnected, yet free-floating swarm of small production teams, the leaves. Each leaf has a specific, clear mission, and every part of that small, manageable leaf knows what its role is. Every organelle of the leaf knows every other organelle by name.

When individual leaves fall or are blown away by a strong wind, the rest survive and carry on with the greater task. Information is accessible in every cell in the form of DNA. Communication passes easily and without delay from membrane to membrane. The system is intimate, alert, and aware. And taken together, the entire "corporation" of leaves, trunk, and root working together, but with local autonomy, contribute to a glorious whole.

This is all very metaphorical, I know. But the point is that large enterprises can achieve their objectives if they are organizationally structured along the lines of a tree, with strong support from the center plus small, intimate teams that know their jobs and have the tools to do them well.

If anything, demassification is demystification. It takes that which was secret and seen only by the priesthood of central controllers and ushers them into the light to be poked, pulled, tugged at, and teased by everyone in the company. When power is held at the center, those on the outskirts are in the dark. When power is shared, the whole enterprise lights up with knowledge and motivation.

Demass is not necessarily elegant. Centralization, with its supertechnologies, global strategies, and pyramidal architecture, is undoubtedly more elegant — and wrong. A huge central warehouse, stuffed to the gills with inventory that may not be used for years is elegant — and a waste. I love to watch all the movers and pickers and sorters at work in an automated warehouse; it is a technological joy. But we're better off without these joys. There is elegance in handling and storing things efficiently, but it's a far, far better thing not to warehouse at all.

In Japan, managers seldom sit back and ooh and ahh at sleek global concepts. They have little time for that; besides, generalizations stunt inquiry. Japan has a healthy disdain for know-it-alls, people who have the answers before they are told the questions. I'm with them. After years of exposure to the grandiose and elegant schemes of central megacontrollers, I doubt that such elegance is a virtue. To be effective, demassification must simplify by taking something huge, unwieldy, and inaccessible and fashioning it into something sleek, malleable, and easily understood.

Demass is both an attitude and a process. The attitude is that central top-down controls simply don't work as well as an integrated, empowered work force. It is that smaller is quicker, better, faster, more flexible, and even more intelligent.

Demassification is part and parcel of a lot of other ideas making the manufacturing rounds:

- When author Richard J. Schonberger calls for world-class manufacturing by insisting that "line people get first crack at problem solving, before staff experts," he is really describing the autonomy of demassification.[1]
- Likewise, when Schonberger calls for multiple points of information access, multiple workstations instead of a single, sacred doorway to the company mainframe or mini, he is really talking demassification.
- When Tom Peters rails against the tendency of top managers to try to control everything, when success lies instead in the opposite direction, of facilitating the talents of associates, he is getting at the central dynamic of demassification.[2]
- When Robert Reich calls for a new kind of corporation, an "enterprise web," combining the power of the

large corporation and the flexibility of the small, he is talking demassification.[3]

- And when Robert Tomasko, in *Downsizing*, calls for reducing the massive corporation to workable size, he too is talking about demassification.[4]

The process of demassification is, above all, one of simplification. It involves reducing the need for corporate staff and unnecessary layers of management. It involves cutting overhead allocations to the bone, taking a huge entity and learning to see it in new ways, and creating intimate, entrepreneurial businesses, running on their autonomous systems. It means pushing decision-making power down to the level where people actually know what is going on and are involved in the doing.

If that definition sounds suspiciously like the core of total quality management, it's because the two concepts are 100 percent mutually compatible. Demassification is to organizational structure and information flow what total quality management is to continuous improvement in all areas of an enterprise.

In the case of IBM, decentralization often means reformatting current operations into new "autonomous" divisions or groups (they call them autonomous, but their actual autonomy is debatable) and shifting employees from one place to the next to minimize complacency and keep people challenged. The idea is interesting, but disconcerting, and a little confusing to the people, especially those who don't want to relocate. Under demass, people are moved around for honest-to-goodness business reasons, such as moving talented top-tier managers out of corporate headquarters and into the operations trenches.

Kenichi Ohmae, chief of McKinsey & Co.'s Tokyo office and author of *The Art of Japanese Business*, writes that the breakup of world headquarters into more flexible, more manageable regional headquarters is key to the new world of global competition. He calls it "decomposing." Companies that decompose, he says, recognize that they cannot keep their ablest managers at home, at the tip of the pyramid; they must put them where they can do the most good, at the local level, where profits are made.

According to Ohmae, "Decomposing the corporate center into several regional headquarters is fast becoming an essential part of almost every successful company's transition to global competitor status. It is a trend that makes good management sense. And it is consistent with recent developments in Europe, in North America as it moves toward the U.S.-Canada-Mexico trade agreement, and in Asia, where the economies of the newly industrialized countries are rapidly integrating with Japan's."[5]

Creating a "street of shops" from a large corporation requires a redefinition of the individual department or function as a "business" and the redefinition of every worker as an entrepreneur, motivated to make a success of the business of which he or she is a part. The success of the macro-enterprise thus depends on the ability of each of its component micro-enterprises to make a profit.

For each micro-enterprise to make a profit, managers and line workers must be free to act wisely in the company's interest. Senior executives who doubt the ability of line workers to absorb the intricacies of corporate strategy are in for a surprise. Though strategy may be a challenge to define and adopt, it must be simplicity itself to explain. Indeed, the surest sign of a superior strategy is that it has the ring of common sense.

Demassification means downsizing and revitalizing information services and moving the function to departmental personal computers and workstations. It means linking teams together to form an interactive, cooperative culture, dedicated to group success through individual excellence. It means creating business units that are crystal clear on both customer focus and product focus — units with performance accountability (spelled out, and in writing) that is in sync with this focus. Demassification means entrusting to those employees who are closest to customers (both internal and external) the mission, responsibility, fact-gathering capability, information tools, and practical incentives to solve business problems.

Who should demassify? Right now, U.S. industry teeters midway between central controls and some hybrid of decentralization. It is, as yet, an undemassified world. My surveys tell me that well under 15 percent of *Fortune* 1000 manufacturers have even a single business unit that meets my criteria for demassification. These are the first days of demassification, the dawn, if you will.

Not every company is a candidate for demassification. You have to be big, for openers. Because you can't demass what isn't massive to begin with, small- to medium-sized companies can undertake all sorts of other worthwhile manufacturing programs, such as JIT (just-in-time), TQM (total quality management), and EI (employee involvement). Small companies may have their own set of problems, but big companies' biggest problem is keeping mass from killing them.

Demass is also not for companies that cannot muster the commitment to invest in training a new kind of work force. Demass is probably the worst thing you could do if you have workers who aren't (or who shouldn't be) high school graduates. And it is not for companies whose managers can only see harm coming from sharing power and maliciously comply by implementing empowerment programs, knowing they are bound to fail.

Companies that need demassifying are large companies that perceive they are in trouble. Companies that, with ample reason, are fighting a losing battle to improve total cycle time, product quality, customer satisfaction, and inventory efficiency.

Demassification is the route to take for companies desperately needing to shorten communication lines, accelerate decision making, cut costs, revitalize worker participation and above all, get products to market faster.

But "street of shops" is anarchy! That's the reaction I get from a lot of senior executives who have heard only a capsule description of demassification. They envision a "de-hierarchized" company in which the CEO stands behind barbed wire watching the corporate "inmates" driving the company into chaos and insolvency on the crest of a wave of uninformed initiatives, unsupervised accounting, duplication of effort, nonstandard standards multiplying like rabbits, and complete capitulation to the whims of a work force drunk with "empowerment."

I think that sounds terrible, too. But it's not what I've been describing. I have described demass as the democratization of the corporation. A demassified corporation is composed of scores or even hundreds of individual "businesses." In each of these businesses, everyone contributing to the business's bottom line should have a say in designing processes. This "democracy" is not there because it is enlightened or fair. It's there because democracy works better than dictatorship. It's more efficient. It's more responsive. It's faster.

In any given job in your organization, the reigning expert is the person who currently has that job. No one is better positioned to do that job well. No one is better positioned to deliver a higher level of customer satisfaction than the person dealing with the individual internal or external customer. That person should have a voice in how the process is conducted. That "voice" is democracy. It does not mean that workers on the floor are always right, or that supervisory responsibilities are stripped away from first-line managers or their managers. Demass is not violent upheaval. It does not mean the guillotine for managers. It is "street of shops," after all, not "blood in the streets." Managers do not become obsolete under a demassified regime. In fact, they are more necessary than ever, but their role is changed. They stop being conductors, and start being orchestrators.

Demass is not without risks. It is loaded with risks. Outbreaks of employee enthusiasm, and business units running off half-cocked, are the kinds of things that can get out of hand. Attempting demass even on a small scale risks upsetting a company's organizational applecart. Companies don't tend to do that unless the apples in the cart are so wormy and rotten no one cares if it's overturned.

As with any course change, the specifics of demassification can go awry. The wrong person may be put in charge of the wrong team. Newly empowered people will, from time to time, do dumb things. Make no mistake: people who are ill-trained or ill-equipped — by nature or by management — to assume decision-making responsibility will kill your business.

To forestall the possibility of your company's degenerating into anarchy, managers must do what they have done since the days of Attila — manage. Managers are still the goal setters of demassified companies. No question: when managers fail in this function of goal setting, motivating, and evaluating, anarchy will result. More to the point, they must institute some form of ordered function deployment so that the attempt to demassify does not dissolve into chaos.

You will find, overnight, that the performance measurements or metrics you once relied on don't work any more; new ones must be designed quickly. The operational levers of your company are subtly different now, and have to be mastered. The same is true of your company's financial levers.

These are the questions that you and your top management team will inevitably be poring over:

- Should we retain overall coordination of order entry, purchasing, financial accounting, etc. at the corporate level, or handle it at the division, plant, or independent business-unit level?
- How many demassified business units should we test-run?
- What is the best way to inculcate a sense of what is appropriate?
- How much latitude for error should be given?
- How much authority is appropriate for a demassified business unit?
- How completely should each business unit control its own information-processing systems?
- Should we have information services impose standard security and backup procedures or simply try to keep ahead of what emerges?
- How do we promote success internally?
- How do we measure success?
- As this process starts taking hold and working, how soon do we demassify additional business units?

Demassification requires an open mind and more power sharing than many of today's CEOs are inclined to cultivate. For you at the top, it is less about telling and more about listening; less about preaching, and more about learning. And there's a funny thing about the learning process — we don't always know where an idea leads once we act on it. It takes practice, error, immersion, and the occasional total loss of perspective for us to find our way, to suddenly gain a truer perspective.

The challenge is to give managers at the lowest levels a solid measure of responsibility. That may mean allowing, even encouraging mistakes early on. So brace yourself. The ride will be exhilarating, but it will also be rough.

The ride is worth the cost, though, because demass offers simplicity, logic, quick, visible results, and a sense of personal excitement, fulfillment, and rejuvenation that inspires the entire company, from people on the lowliest shop floor to those sitting in the penthouse corner office.

You CEOs who earned your stripes the hard way — remember what excited and motivated you most to become a CEO? What was it again? Wasn't it the chance to run a company the way you wanted? Wasn't that what drove you, made you give your very best? What if that kind of enthusiasm could be injected into all your workers? Wouldn't that be something to see?

For those of you still unconvinced, or who see demassification as a diminution of your role, here's a final incentive: demass doesn't take away the company you are now running; it gives you a whole bunch of new companies to run. And making a whole bunch of companies successful should tap into your true potential.

4

Demassification and Downsizing Information Systems

Central information services, or MIS, or IS — whatever a company calls it — has become an enclave focused on new hardware platforms, intracompany communication protocols, open systems, hierarchical data standards, and the like. In many large companies, keeping what worked in the past working in the present takes over 75 percent of total software staff resources. Whatever happened to data processing's role of helping operations execute?

There's a new job at most large corporations that didn't exist 15 years ago — the chief information officer, or CIO. It's a position of the 1980s, that might not make it past the 1990s. It is a top-tier job — CIOs usually report directly to the chief executive officer. The position should not be confused with the vice president-management information services, who actually runs a company's data processing services.

The CIO is an executive, usually with a small staff, whose concern is the asset management of corporate information. The CIO is the guardian, the overseer, of the information that the corporation runs on. The CIO's concerns include sabotage, data integrity, confidentiality, and planning for the future. Whereas the head of MIS runs the day-to-day data processing operations, the CIO is in charge of the big picture, the long term. The CIO's grasp of future developments must be unerring. The position seems custom-built to bear the load of megatons of blame.

It's tough to be a chief information officer these days. You can count the successful ones on one hand. Technological changes never let up; they are like an avalanche that continually buries the corporate cabin under new mountains of snow. Peers in senior management never have a clue what the CIO is talking about, yet they are generous in pointing their fingers at the CIO when something goes wrong. Technological evolution forces CIOs into the role of change agents, and that is never a safe role in any organization.

A recent poll of *Fortune* 500 CIOs in *Information Week* revealed that retirement is the least frequently given reason for CIOs leaving their jobs.[1] And manufacturing was cited as the second unlikeliest sector for CIO longevity; only distribution saw more CIO demotions and dismissals. Problems run so deep at so many companies that appointing someone as the next CIO is often a feat of planned scapegoating.

If you aspire to getting the CIO title, good luck, and be careful. When your new colleagues pat you on the back to congratulate you on your new job, you'd best double-check to see that they aren't attaching a bull's-eye.

Is it any wonder that many corporate executives on a fast track ruefully consider that CIO really stands for "career is over"? Failure stalks the great blinking mainframe chambers clutching a sharp scythe, looking for bright-eyed professionals to mow down. And the look on its face is one of delight because it knows that the mission of the chief information executive, as currently defined in the large corporation, is virtually impossible. That is, unless large companies take a radically new tack.

Demassification, as I have said, is not possible without the convergence of two processes. The first is organizational restructuring, the radical decentralization of large companies, with maximum autonomy, into many small independent business units. The objective is to take a large, unwieldy company and to restructure it using the "street-of-shops" model until each business unit operates as a motivated, competent entity linked to the whole through effectively networked management.

The other process, downsizing of information-processing technology, flows naturally from the first. Technology downsizing is best expressed as the idea of eliminating or reducing mainframes and minicomputers and replacing them with networks of powerful personal computers and technical workstations. It is the movement of applications from centralized mainframes to distributed smaller systems. Information technology downsizing is really the democratization of computing: power to the people!

A "street of shops" is the goal, while organizational restructuring and information-processing technology downsizing are the means to achieve that goal. Finding an optimal way to execute the two processes, with maximum benefits and minimum liabilities, is what this chapter is about.

In 1970, large systems computers and peripherals accounted for 11 percent of all durable equipment bought by businesses. By 1989 that figure had risen to 51 percent.[2] During that period, manufacturing grew healthily, at about 3 percent annually. But in the service sector information services expenditures went through the roof. More than three-quarters of all information-processing technology investments today are made by service companies. Technological advances on the service side led naturally to advances on the manufacturing side. Many service businesses never had to downsize their systems because they were never "upsized" to begin with.

The main thrust of the personal computer revolution to date has not been in the area of manufacturing operations. Indeed, manufacturing operations today remains one of the last major strongholds of massified information. Now it's manufacturing's turn to learn of the benefits of downsized information-processing technology.

COMPUTERS AND DEMASS

Downsizing of information-processing technology is not really an option; it is an inevitability. Large systems create an immovable status quo that freezes management in its tracks. Smaller systems enhance a company's ability to react. Applications are already being handed down from big systems to little. Large systems gobble up too much of a corporation's resources, both dollars and people. Smart management is pulling the plug and putting resources where they can best affect the bottom line.

The benefits of information-processing technology downsizing are quickly apparent — decreased cost at every stage (hardware, software, maintenance, personnel), flexibility, user-friendliness, and faster implementation of applications. With ease of use comes improved productivity. Eventually, downsized information-processing technology will mean a new kind of information-services department, one that communicates more effectively with other departments and is more closely linked with the overall productivity and profitability of a company's line operations.

The downside is also apparent. We don't yet have true "open systems" compatibility between all microcomputers; we have, instead, a quagmire of hardware and software incompatibilities. Without open systems or clear universal standards, the door is open to end-user anarchy, with no two business units speaking the same language. Meanwhile, amid the turmoil of converting from large, remote systems to small, local ones, there is the likelihood of severe alienation and disaffection among information-services workers.

Companies that eventually demassify don't start out huge. And those that are properly demassified may not have to rely on computers. Many American industry representatives returning from Japan have observed that there aren't nearly as many computers in the Japanese as there are here.

For that matter, you don't absolutely need computers or software to manufacture. But practically speaking, nearly every company uses them extensively. One estimate is that two-thirds of corporate desktops now have computers on them.

Corporations with centralized control or centralized locations of most activities are most likely to have centralized computing. Corporations trying to get away from top-heavy central control most likely use or plan to use downsized systems. So how, exactly, does a demassified company use computers differently from an undemassified company?

PLUSES AND MINUSES OF CENTRALIZED COMPUTING

Why mainframes? Centralization of information derives historically not from the dictatorial whims of top management but from the happenstance of technology. Early computers had to be centralized because they were (and are) huge and expensive, and needed a lot of special care and feeding. Mainframe computers may have, in fact, laid the groundwork for massive centralization. Their power to store, sort, and execute opened the door to truly massive corporate operations.

Before the arrival of the big boxes in the wake of World War II, there was a natural cap on the size a corporation could aspire to, dictated by the amount of paper and information it could competently process. The rise of the mega-corporation followed closely on the heels of the development of the burly batch sorters. The development of computers signaled the onset of what Alvin Toffler called "The Third Wave," the information age.[3] But while data was plentiful, true information in the form of usable, shared, and communicated data was perhaps scarcer than ever.

Mainframe computers in most large companies are the heart of that company's operations: shrines of data and strongholds of corporate power. They did not set out to monopolize a company's information power and shut others out. That was simply the logical consequence of mainframe architecture, which was necessarily housed in a single location, and attended by a select group who understood and could communicate in the computer's arcane language.

Wouldn't it be great if a single computer could drive all of a company's many sites? That is, after all, the idea of central computing. It sounds elegant, but in reality it never works out that way. People and systems do not thrive under central control and fare even worse under remote central control.

Information-processing technology downsizing was really not possible a decade ago. Corporations used mainframe computers and built their own applications, since generalized software packages were expensive and not widely available. Many of the biggest changes enabling corporations to work more flexibly occurred in the information systems area. Since the early days, hardware costs have plummeted. Both the cost per byte of memory and the cost per byte of storage have fallen like an anvil. Today there are desktop computers that are larger in memory, larger in storage, and faster than their mainframe ancestors—while costing only a fraction as much.

Software inflexibility. The real change, however, has been in the area of commercially packaged ("canned" and "off-the-shelf") software. These packages are typically developed by independent companies with software programming specialists who are extremely knowledgeable in their application area: MRP II, human resources, etc. The applications are built to appeal to and work for many different kinds of companies. For a packaged software company to succeed, it must sell to many different companies. To meet the needs of a wide variety of companies, the package must be flexible in the extreme.

Where mainframe software has been predominantly designed to serve a company's present and specific needs, off-the-shelf software is normally designed to include a breadth of features that companies can use or not use, as their needs and requirements change.

Mainframe software is designed and maintained by a few in-house professionals. They are talented, but their task is usually determined by managerial edict. Independent software developers, by contrast, are businesspeople, entrepreneur/technologists who know they will succeed richly if they can deliver programs that excel in flexibility, features, power, and speed.

An analogy can be made to advertising. In-house advertising is usually quite serviceable, but most companies understand that the artists and writers and strategists at outside agencies bring more firepower to the task at hand. Compared to these highly paid hotshots, in-house advertising professionals or software developers can't help coming across as a little drab.

Most software delivered in off-the-shelf packages is easily tailored to fit different companies' evolving needs. Conversely, customizing or updating in-house mainframe software on the fly is like trying to redirect traffic in a stampeding buffalo herd. You can do it, but it sure isn't easy. Every large system keeps a list of changes it plans to make "in the next major upgrade," and that can take years.

Restricted access. I called large systems shrines, and the problem with shrines is that they require a specialized priesthood. And that is exactly what centralized computing got. It got a class of people who were supposed to be revealers but who instead were often concealers, drawing a curtain around themselves and the mysteries they guarded. The curtain was a natural consequence of the technology's difficulty, the magical nature of data in electronic flight. As data became the coin of the corporate realm, those who had data held power, and those who did not, had none.

In the early years of corporate computing, the great fear was of a computer crash, downtime, and lost data. A complete breakdown could mean death. Abercrombie & Fitch, the upscale outdoors retailer, had to go out of business when its computer lost its entire accounts receivable data in the 1970s.

With the passage of time, reliability problems have eased, and access has become the primary concern of centralized information services. Companies used to worry that their computers would blow up; now, with computers controlling and costing so much, and cooperating with us so little, we sometimes wish they would blow up.

Many CEOs have chafed at the restrictive flow of information in their companies, or complained that the data, gathered far away, bore little resemblance to reality. Many a CEO has taken a backseat to managers who had better and faster access to data, and gripped it tightly, and used it for their own advancement, or to protect their fiefdoms.

High cost. A computer scientist once remarked that it is odd that we complain about the "runaway costs and cost overruns" of our computer systems, but we never seem to boast of the "runaway benefits and benefit overruns" of having them on our side.

The reason, of course, is that the costs are so obvious on the balance sheet and so painful. For three decades, big system computing has continued to cast about for more things to suck into its vast data base of stored electronic signals. Consequently, every large system has continued to grow, and with that growth, so too have costs skyrocketed.

Way back in 1983 it was estimated that Department of Defense software maintenance alone cost between $2.5 and $4 billion annually. I doubt if even the most stringent fiscal conservatives would want to know what that figure is like today.

It is estimated by market research companies that 80 percent of electronic data processing cycle time spent on a large computer is spent not on crunching numbers but on maintenance chores, that is, keeping its internal processes shipshape. That figure, 80 percent, or even half that figure, would be unacceptable in any other activity of modern industry. But in centralized information-services departments we shrug it off as the "cost of doing business."

As a system grows, and as the demands placed on the system grow, so does the continuing cost of maintaining it. This is especially true of large system software maintenance, done by large teams of programmers, that change frequently, so no single member of which knows the full story. Large system code is like an ever-changing river — its contour and design is in too much constant flux for us ever to become "expert" about it.

Corporate internal software development and subsequent maintenance is always experimental, always "custom-made" and thus expensive to create and ultra-expensive to maintain. Complex mainframe operating systems muddle the situation even more.

Big companies have acknowledged the high cost of centralized computing, but not always in the right way. An evolving expression of it is information services outsourcing. Information-processing technology is evolving rapidly at the same moment that companies are experiencing extreme pressure to cut costs. The solution? Farm out information-processing work to third parties. These MIS partners are not cheap, but they can save companies about 10 to 30 percent on their MIS costs annually. They absorb the costs of keeping up to date technologically, and computers are their business.

Outsourcing demand, according to one report, is expected to double from 1991 to 1995. About 2 to 3 percent of the *Fortune* 500 have already outsourced some or all of their information-processing systems. By 1995, this percentage will have vaulted to 20 percent.[4]

Outsourcing of information services is not a bad idea. In fact, of all the partnering schemes to come down the pike in the past few years, outsourcing makes sense. But it has one serious drawback: it does not change the net effect of how information flows in your company.

So if your company decides to hand off its computer chores to a third party, insist not just on transferring the chore, but also on downsizing the way the chore is done. But in rethinking the way you want information to flow to and from your independent business units, you are likely to find that inexpensive technology already exists for handling the vast majority of information-services tasks. You may save even more money by keeping your data at home but working with it in a different, demassified way.

While internally developed software costs are rising, hardware costs just keep tumbling. Between 1960 and 1990 the price of computing power in America fell by a factor of 6,000 (in real dollars). That drop followed a descending pattern of 25 to 30 percent per year. The future appears to have more of the same in store. What is striking is the comparative rates of estimated decline. Today, powerful micro-based computers (e.g., powerful personal computers and technical workstations) offer processing at unit costs up to 100 times lower than large minicomputers and mainframes. (See figure, p. 72.)

Local-area networks, often referred to by the acronym LANs, allow these personal computers and workstations to be connected at modest cost using standard equipment available from a wide variety of vendors. Common data storage facilities on local-area networks rival, in capacity, those on the largest mainframes. In the near future, microcomputers' unit cost advantage — some technologists use the yardstick cost per million instructions per second, or MIPS, for comparative purposes — will continue to accelerate.

A sure sign that the cost advantage of microcomputers over traditional mainframes and minicomputers is real is

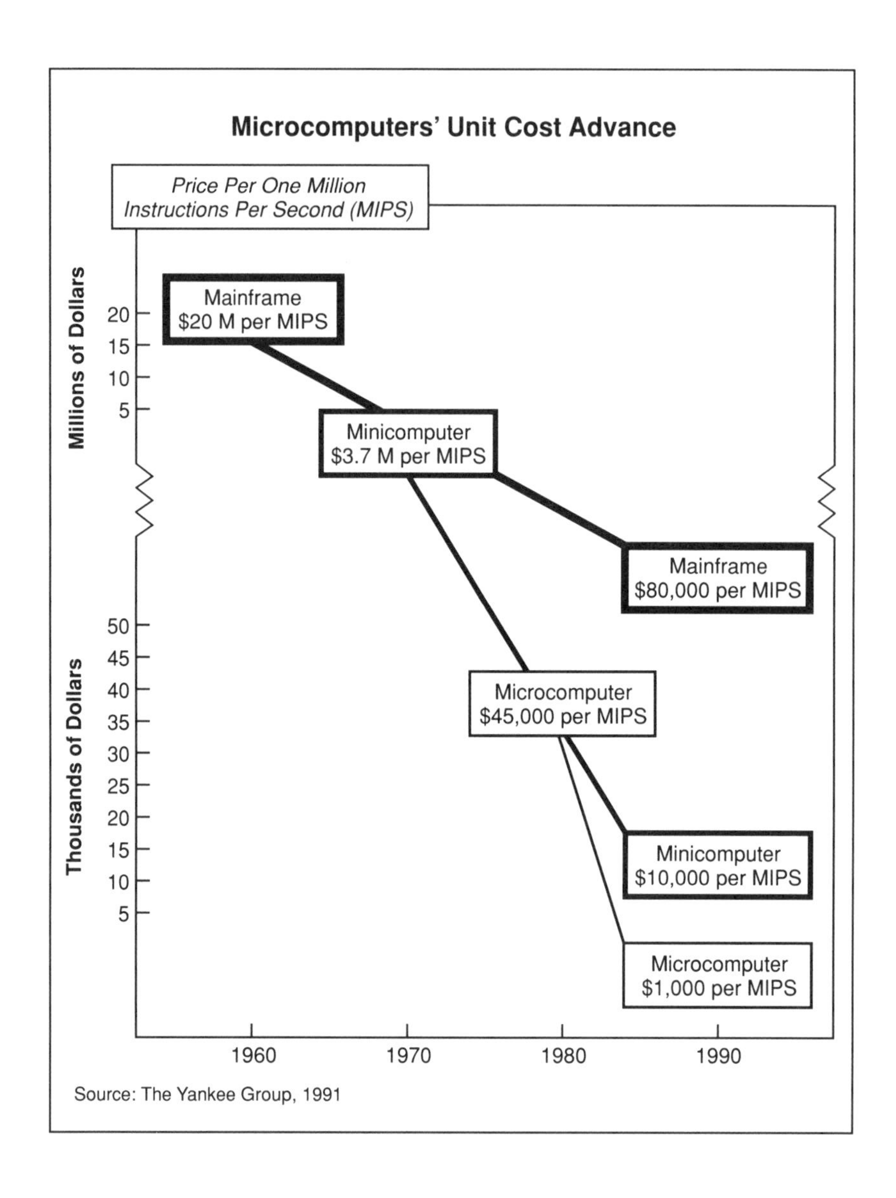

when Wall Street heavy hitters start issuing position papers about downsizing. A May 1991 Salomon Brothers report on downsizing carried strong quotes from Will Zachmann, then an analyst for Canopus Research and a well-known observer of the computer industry. "Downsizing is inevitable because it enhances the enterprise's ability to react," Zachmann said. "There is absolutely nothing traditional systems can do that microprocessor-based alternatives can't do at a substantially lower cost."

The Salomon Brothers report concluded: "We have used various approaches to describe the dramatic changes taking place. The bottom line is always the same — downsizing will realign the industry's power structure."[5]

An advantage often overlooked when comparing personal computers to mainframes is the cost of disposal. Mainframes depreciate rapidly in value, and are difficult to off-load onto secondary markets. It is common for a multimillion-dollar system to go for as little as 10 percent of its original cost after less than eight years of use, or, you may have to pay to have it hauled away as scrap.

Personal computer systems, by contrast, are composed primarily of parts. When something becomes outdated, such as a motherboard, a master chip, or device of any kind, it can often be upgraded on the spot. Failing that, you can usually sell the parts for at least a quarter of what you paid. Or you can donate them to a school and take the tax write-off. Personal computers are absurdly cheap. The dawn of demassification is also the dawn of computer disposability.

EIGHT OBJECTIONS TO INFORMATION-PROCESSING TECHNOLOGY DOWNSIZING

It is easy to understand why MIS professionals are resistant to the kind of downsizing I see as inevitable. I count eight reasons:

1. **MIS has a good thing going.** Over the past decade, information services departments in large corporations have grown at a rapid rate and become more centralized. Even when other departments have had hiring freezes imposed on them, information services has continued to grow.
2. **Who wants to be profit driven?** It's nice to be a special case on the corporate flowchart, a department that does not have to show a profit at year's end. In fact, information-services promotions are usually based on factors running counter to the bottom line: how many programmers you have under your control; what long-term, complex projects you are heading up; what special expertise you have that no one else has. It is more like a college campus than a business. Information services is so isolated from everyday business realities that many professionals have never set foot in an operating department.
3. **Whom do we work for again?** Many large information-services departments have close relationships with big computer vendors. When the downsizing revolution occurred, these vendors misled and misdirected information-services departments, saying that PCs were a passing trend. As a result, the revolution passed by some of our biggest corporations, except at the grass-roots, non–information-services level. A lot of high-tech marvels became ironically obsolete.
4. **Not Invented Here!** The NIH Syndrome is simple arrogance — if we didn't create it, how good could it be? Information-services departments turn up their noses at standard software packages they can't tinker

with endlessly. Here are people almost unbelievably divorced from the everyday realities of doing business, claiming that off-the-shelf, market-tested software could not possibly meet business requirements.

5. **A passion for antiquity.** It amazes me how inefficient in-house software has become. Many new computer science graduates come out intent on using outdated machine-level or first generation languages, because their professors told them that the newer, more efficient languages were intellectually inferior. Even more amazing, their supervisors let them get away with it.
6. **Let's reinvent the wheel.** There is a culture among many information-services departments where people simply don't choose to work as teams. People hoard information and expertise, withholding important input until it is too late. "I know something you don't know," appears to be the rallying cry.
7. **Fear of fading.** Deep down, information-services people know the writing is on the wall. Large systems technology has had its day, and a new day is dawning, and they're not part of it, and that scares the heck out of them. Having spent years mastering the old technology, how can they catch up to the new?
8. **Fear of firing.** If downsized information-processing technology saves a fortune in development and maintenance costs, what happens to all the people who have been doing the developing and maintaining? Information-services people should be scared, because only the flexible and the most business-minded will survive.

WHERE DOWNSIZED INFORMATION-PROCESSING TECHNOLOGY IS HEADING

The network *is* the computer. People who follow the growth of networking technologies sometimes lump networks in with computer peripherals. But my view is that networks — LANs (local-area networks), WANs (wide-area networks), data bridges, and other connectivity technologies — are not secondary in importance to computers themselves. Indeed, it makes sense to think of the networks as the heart of the computing process. The network *is* the computer.

The original computers did not network. They were large and centralized. If you wanted a problem solved, you went to the computer. But with the invention of the microchip, computers began a steady march toward miniaturization. From yesterday's humble 8-bit desktop personal computers to today's powerful 32-bit machines, users have embraced the accessibility of the desktop.

But, from the onset of this miniaturization revolution, sharing information from machine to machine has been a problem. In the early 1980s, offices with more than one personal computer used a "sneakernet": someone who came in after hours and ran from PC to PC, putting a new floppy disk in each, including all changes made that day. Primitive, but it did achieve a level of basic information sharing.

In 1982, however, the Novell Corporation introduced its first electronic networking product — wires that interconnected personal computers, and software to make it all work. By using Novell's networking product, called NetWare, people could share a common printer and data base, and everybody could use the same software simultaneously.

It is possible to claim that "the network is the computer" because the flexibility, accessibility, and functionality of a networked system have come to outweigh in significance simple storage and data processing.

Mainframes will not go away without a fight. The installed base at large corporations is big and ingrained. A wealth of entrenched software already exists for these machines, and corporate information services departments are loath to downsize to smaller systems. For the moment, too many "mission-critical" corporate functions that can shut a company down if they go haywire are still the province of large systems.

In the long term, the mainframe will go the way of the dinosaur. In the short term, its strength will lie more in size and raw power than in unit sales. Increasingly, the mainframe will assume more limited roles, as the beast of burden for huge data loads, as specialty tools in research, and as giant switches for zillions of little computers.

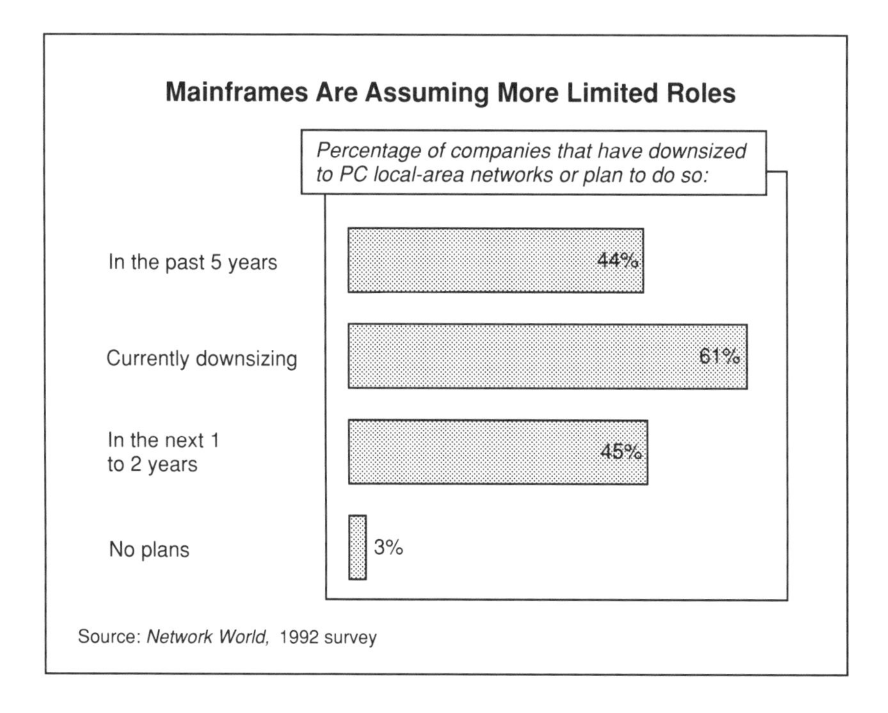

Before the turn of the century, microchip technology — PCs and workstations — will rule the roost. While networking is no longer in its infancy (over a quarter of all personal computers in the United States are now networked) it still cannot be described as mature. Networked personal computers are easy to use, very affordable, and can be installed one piece at a time. The writing is on the wall, or via networking, through the wall. The network is the computer. We will never work the old way again.

A computer or a toy? A few years ago, it was appropriate for computer specialists to snicker at the idea of information-systems downsizing. In their view, downsizing had already occurred, when Digital Equipment and other companies developed minicomputers to achieve on a decentralized scale what mainframes had been doing the previous decade. Surely, the latest wrinkle on the scene, the desktop personal computer, was not claiming that it could do what the humongous IBM, Burroughs, and Sperry mainframes did!

In a sense they were right to be apprehensive. In the early 1980s, before hard drives made significant storage possible, before networking made significant information sharing possible, before more generous operating memory made significant work loads possible, the PC seemed a brave little toy, nothing more. It was not even a threat to dedicated word processors, much less a serious computing tool.

But change came quickly and in unprecedented waves. The desktop computer grew in size and power. Microprocessors — the "computer on a chip" that revolutionized computer technology and made personal computers run — grew steadily in power and functionality, from the Intel- and Motorola-designed microprocessor that powered the early IBM PC and Apple computers, to today's microprocessors that operate at breathtaking speed and power the fastest network file servers.

Intel's next generation of microprocessors, the 586, reportedly operates at speeds up to 100 million instructions per second. Additionally, Intel is now discussing a turn-of-the-century microprocessor chip dubbed "Micro 2000," which would contain upwards of 60 million transistors, or at least 20 times as many as the upcoming 586, and blaze through 2 billion calculations per second, more than all but a few of today's supercomputers do.

Beyond today's chips is the prospect of multiprocessor-driven machines — personal computers with a raft of chips lashed together to create an electronic brain more powerful than current mainframes, while still fitting on a desktop. New "flash memory" chips created in a joint Intel/Sharp project promise to produce, by the year 2000, a computer that weighs as little as two pounds, is only a half-inch thick, runs on a battery good for 200 hours of operation, and costs only $200. Some of the computers based on these chips won't look like computers but will appear in manifestations as unlikely as pen-sized tape recorders and electronic novels. Flash chips may even eventually replace disk drives as conventional storage technologies.

There is even this tantalizing possibility: that microprocessors of the future may be micro-lasers, invisibly small units that transmit not at the "plodding" speeds of long-distance networks but 3,000 times faster, at the speed of light!

Software support for microprocessor-based machines, in the form of increasingly open and sturdy operating platforms like Microsoft Windows, OS/2, and UNIX, offer flexibility and "grow-ability," enabling companies to build powerful, even world-class information systems "one bite at a time."

The architecture is wide open. You can crack open a personal computer and modify it any way you like, with telecommunications cards, coprocessors, a wide array of storage devices, input devices like mouses and pens, extra memory, scanners, faxes, you name it. Since the operating systems are fairly standardized, a ton of software is available, either off the shelf or created from off-the-shelf development tools. And best of all, they are so user-friendly that a computer illiterate can operate one.

Has the toy somehow replaced the mainframe? How can this be? What's kept this news from reaching the top echelons of corporate America?

Platforms and systems. Personal computer hardware platforms have evolved rapidly and remarkably — a tremendous advance for office technology. Perhaps even more important, however, is the revolution that has been occurring in software. In every software applications category (word processing, spreadsheets, database management, etc.) microcomputer-based software technology has grown and expanded exponentially. Buyers no longer have to worry about getting "the best" product in their niche because so many are excellent that it's hard to go wrong.

But the critical area in computers today is neither hardware platforms nor application software. It is, rather, computer operating systems, the undergirding that forms the base of everything computers do.

When trying to understand operating systems, let me warn you, there is a wonderful opportunity to get very confused, very quickly. The reason is that the computer industry, and all of us who regularly use computers, are currently engaged in a stormy debate about which operating system is the wave of the future. Computer users want to know which operating system will move us from the bad old days of proprietary systems — computers that could only run what was made specifically for them — toward an elusive nirvana called "open systems."

Since the day the first computer was plugged in, one dream above all others has guided, and at times tormented, software developers: the idea of universal compatibility, of "open systems," whereby all computers would use stable, publicly defined, or "standard" interfaces that enable them to talk to each other and use the same software, no matter what brand or size.

The idea of open systems is to the computer industry what a back-porch light is to flying insects — dazzling, irresistible, and not a little dangerous. Every computer hardware vendor would like to put out the most open machine. The problem is that individual computer vendors don't get to define what "open" means. We consumers of computers do. While all hardware vendors want to be "open," they all want to be open on their own terms. The result has been a bewildering combination of half-open, half-proprietary machines and operating systems on the market.

Which software platform? In cooperation with IBM, Microsoft Corporation, the new kid on the block that has become a software giant, created the standard (most popular) operating system for the IBM personal computer and compatibles, MS-DOS (Microsoft Disk Operating System). IBM and Microsoft have since had disagreements, and IBM has been pushing hard, and with limited success to date, for a newer OS/2 operating system to become the new standard. Microsoft, however, with its "DOS extension" product called Windows, and its highly touted future product called NT, is working hard to keep IBM's OS/2 off most of the playing field.

Apple Computer Corporation, another very successful developer and marketer of personal computers, sells its own unique personal computer noted for its ease of use. Apple's system is non-IBM compatible and has its own proprietary operating system. While the Apple Macintosh is gaining in sales, it is still a distant second to IBM-compatible computers. IBM-compatibles out-ship Macintoshes by 10 to 1.

And IBM compatibles out-ship UNIX-based computers by 100 to 1. Developed years ago by AT&T, UNIX is an operating system used more by engineers than businesspeople. It is the operating system of choice for users of technical workstations. To keep us on our toes, UNIX comes in delightfully different flavors, such as XENIX, AIX, DYNIX, AUX, UNIX V.4, SUN OS, ULTRIX, HP/UX, and DG/UX, depending on which machine it is run on.

Which silicon platform? To make our choices even more interesting, there are two competing hardware architectures, or platforms, to pick from. These are actually two different kinds of microprocessors that work in subtly different ways. The first has been on the market for years and is called a CISC- (Complex Instruction Set Computing) based chip. According to Forrester Research, over 7 million CISC-based computers were shipped in 1990 by over 300 different manufacturers.

The second is newer, and is called a RISC- (Reduced Instruction Set Computing) based chip. Because it has fewer instructions the claim is that RISC is faster then CISC. It is probably fruitless to argue as to which technology is really faster or better. Most personal computers you are familiar with (IBM personal computers and compatibles as well as Apple Macintoshes) are CISC based. Most of the new workstations, including those from Sun Microsystems, Hewlett-Packard, IBM, and Data General, are RISC based.

Following is a summary of worldwide chip consumption in 1991, showing which microprocessors are most popular and prevalent in the marketplace today.

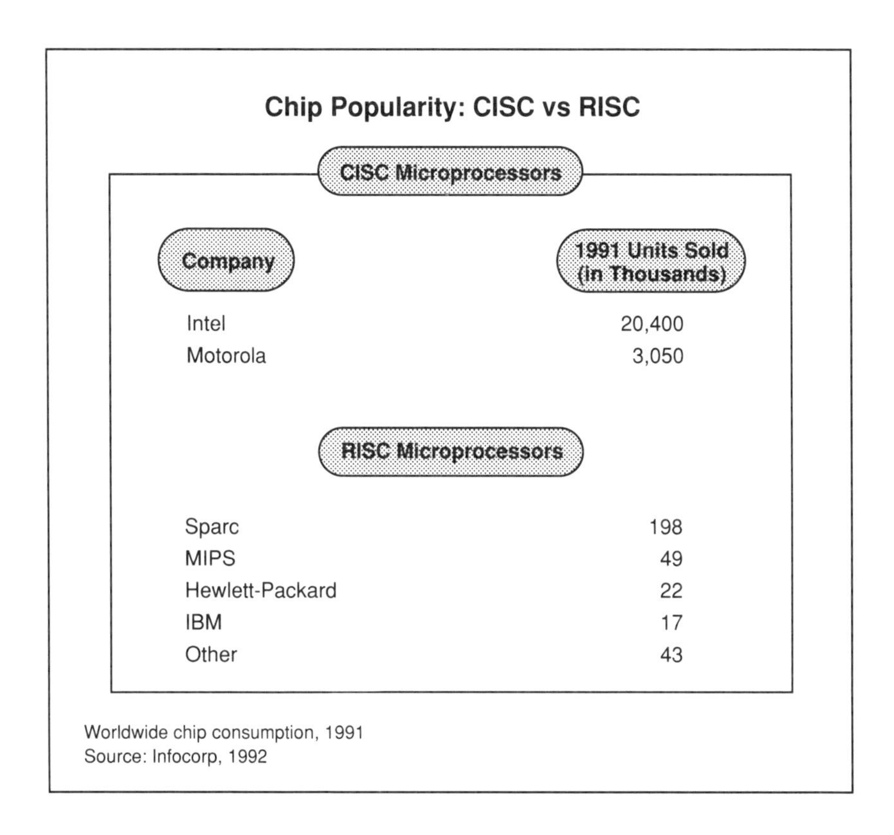

Chip Popularity: CISC vs RISC

Company	1991 Units Sold (In Thousands)
CISC Microprocessors	
Intel	20,400
Motorola	3,050
RISC Microprocessors	
Sparc	198
MIPS	49
Hewlett-Packard	22
IBM	17
Other	43

Worldwide chip consumption, 1991
Source: Infocorp, 1992

Some say that UNIX, which is generally run on RISC-based computers, is the operating system of the future. UNIX is a natural multitasking, multiuser operating system. (In English that means it can do more than one task at a time, with more than one person using it at a time.)

However, DOS, which is generally run on CISC-based computers, has by far the largest installed base. About 90 percent of all desktop computers in the world today run on

CISC chips made by Intel Corporation. DOS is therefore very attractive because of its mountain of high-quality software programs. As of right now, DOS is the favorite of developers and users.

I could go deeper into the multilayers of technology issues, such as which "graphical user interfaces" go with which CISC and RISC systems from which hardware vendors along with the unique advantages of each, but I feel supremely confident that I have sufficiently confused you with high-tech categories and droll acronyms.

Let me try to tidy it all up with a few commonsense observations and conclusions. Open systems are good. Proprietary systems are bad. However, there will surely be more than one open system winner over the next five or so years. Pick any open system winner and move away from proprietary mainframes and minicomputers, and your company will be making a sound long-term financial decision.

THE DAWN OF DOWNSIZED INFORMATION-PROCESSING TECHNOLOGY

When does a breeze become a gale? When does a ripple become a tidal wave? When does a trend become a transformation?

Since 1991, the *Wall Street Journal* has carried numerous front-page stories such as "PC Networks Begin to Oust Mainframes."[6] *Business Week* has written many articles about technology downsizing such as "How Those Mainframes on a Chip Are Changing the Way We Use Computers" and "As Markets and Technology Change, Can IBM Remake Its Culture?"[7] *Harvard Business Review*, *Fortune*, *Forbes*, and *The*

Economist all report frequently on the movement of business computing from "proprietary" mainframes and minicomputers to the newer, faster, cheaper "open" personal computers and workstations.

Charles E. Exley, past chairman and CEO of NCR Corporation, which for many years made a lot of money out of developing and selling proprietary minicomputers, announced that he was transforming the way NCR would do business when he said, "We are on the brink of a major crossover between micros and mainframes. The microprocessor revolution is becoming an irresistible force. Ultimately, every business will want to move from their mainframes to microprocessors."

You probably won't find IBM Corporation or Digital Equipment raving about technology downsizing, or "rightsizing" as some people have termed it. Their business need is to protect huge installed bases of high-margin proprietary minicomputers and mainframes. This makes them unlikely proponents of downsizing.

And you won't find a huge percentage of information-services executives lining up to cheer for the changes under way. They know, however, just as IBM and Digital Equipment do, that a genuine transfer of power is taking place in corporate America. It is passing from the hands of the data processors' "priesthood" into the hands of the people.

The pressures from entrenched hardware vendors, along with resistance from the information-services community, are considerable obstacles for CEOs to overcome. No one likes crossing swords with a giant. But the hardware vendors who are arguing that the day of the mainframe has not passed are wrong. The twilight of the monolithic machine is at hand.

5
Portrait of a Company That's Demassifying

Can a giant think small? Eastman Kodak is making a serious run at it. Its "street-of-shops" organization concept has roused employees' sense of participation, increased flexibility, and reduced costs. They're not there yet, and like most of us, they tend to keep getting drawn back to what used to be comfortable, but they are trying.

Telling chief executives how they should demassify their company can be done rather simply. Simply analyze your corporation's problems, decide that *mass* is a key issue that must be addressed, create a plan to deal with it, shake up top management, announce job classification changes to all 100,000 employees, empower and train everybody, fire everyone who can't get with the new program, put the mainframe computers

---

The company that I run, FOURTH SHIFT Corporation, played a supporting role in this process. Much of my information in this chapter comes from personal interviews with Kodak managers including, but not limited to George Hannye, Frank Zaffino, Kathy Hudson, George Fellows and Jack Philbin.

out with the trash, hose down the information-services people, and call a press conference to announce the dividend hike.

But as every CEO knows, actually instituting changes is never simple. Demassifying a large company is an enormous undertaking. Perhaps the biggest and toughest part of all is the first step — acknowledging that a problem exists and coming to grips with the truths that your company has simply grown too big to function flexibly, and that you as CEO have lost control.

The following is a true story about the balky process that led one of America's greatest companies, Eastman Kodak, to realize that inflexibility and unmanageability would eventually lead to ruin, and what it did to remedy the problem. Kodak was one of the first *Fortune* 500 companies to attempt to recreate itself via structural reorganization and information-processing technology downsizing.

CENTRALIZATION AT EASTMAN KODAK

It was never written in stone that Eastman Kodak was destined for greatness. Established in 1884 as the Eastman Dry Plate and Film Company, the company was the brainchild of one of America's great inventor-industrialists, George Eastman, of Rochester, New York.

Eastman's first camera was a simple, hand-held box with no viewfinder, containing a 100-exposure roll of paper stripping film. You snapped your pictures, then mailed the entire camera, unopened, with a $10 developing fee, to Eastman's company, which then returned the camera, again preloaded. In 1889, Eastman invented transparent film and reorganized his company as the Eastman Kodak Company.

Kodak, he said, was a word he made up himself. "A trademark should be short, vigorous, incapable of being misspelled to an extent that will destroy its identity," he said. "And — in order to satisfy trademark laws — it must mean nothing." Eastman liked the letter *K* — "a short, incisive sort of letter." Thus K had to be the first letter. By moving vowels and consonants around he arrived at a name that today sounds almost Japanese.

His idea was a liberating one for consumers. Up until then photography could only be the province of professionals. Eastman's dry plate photography inventions made it possible for anyone with a steady hand to take pictures. In 1900 he unveiled the Brownie camera, intended for children and priced at one dollar. The slogan: "You push the button — we do the rest." The Brownie used easily removable film, further demystifying the photographic industry. Technology once accessible to only a few was now available to the multitudes, and the multitudes responded.

Eastman Kodak was a company with a phenomenal record for new product development. In addition to transparent film and Brownie cameras, Eastman's company took the three basic colors — yellow, magenta, and cyan — and transposed images of each to create color moving pictures, color film, home movie and slide cameras, color photocopying, compact disk photography, and thousands of other patents.

By 1927 Eastman Kodak had risen to undisputed leadership status within the U.S. photographic industry. Eastman's company had become so massive that in 1924 the one-time bank clerk donated half of his fortune of more than $75 million to the University of Rochester, its Eastman School of Music, and MIT. His largess did not stop there. He was one of the first capitalists to recognize the value of employee involvement, establishing America's first corporate profit-sharing plan.

Eventually, Eastman Kodak's hegemony in the photographic industry came under challenge. The first challenge came from Polaroid Land Camera in 1947, which simplified photography even further by eliminating process laboratories altogether. Polaroid reduced the "total cycle time" of taking a picture from three days to 60 seconds — a revolutionary and, to Eastman Kodak, a shocking advance.

By any definition today, Eastman Kodak Company qualifies as being massive. With 134,000 employees, annual sales of almost $19 billion, and over 175,000 shareholders worldwide, Eastman Kodak figures in the top echelon of just about everything: volume and dollar amount of exports, return on equity, consumer ratings, familiarity, and brand loyalty.

Americans snap 21 million photographs daily — enough for a 29-acre carpet of wallet-size photos, for which Kodak provides most of the film.[1] Eastman Kodak, started on a shoestring a century ago, is today nothing less than a super-company. But in many ways it is also a troubled one. By the 1970s Kodak was feeling the heat of competition in its cash cow business lines. Fuji Film of Japan was making market-share inroads on Kodak's mainstay product line, pulling away about 10 percent of the 50 billion photographs taken yearly.

Massive as Kodak was, with all its market clout, advertising and research and development budgets, administrative synergies, and "economies of scale," and though three-quarters of the world's households still didn't own a camera, Eastman Kodak found itself unable to take advantage.

This situation persisted throughout the 1970s, and the handful of executives who ran Eastman Kodak were puzzled about how to amend the course they were on. It didn't seem to make sense: they had the best laboratories by far; the biggest, the most impressive proprietary mainframe systems; and state-of-the-art warehousing systems that could instantly locate, pick, and retrieve the smallest inventoried item in a gnat's wink. They had one of the most honored and respected consumer brand names in the world. And they recruited some of the brightest and best managers that America's business schools were turning out.

How centralized was Eastman Kodak? In the early days of development on the successful Instamatic camera, the camera was to use a built-in automatic focusing default so that it would automatically take acceptable close-ups, midrange shots, or shots taken at a distance. Engineers, who had invested thousands of hours in the camera, had set the camera on the midrange position. Most pictures, they figured, were midrange, so why not? But before the camera setting got the go-ahead, the corporation's chairman, Alfred Chapman, examined the camera personally and decided that the Instamatic would be set for close-ups. One man's best judgment at the top overruled reams of exhaustive market research from below!

The half-dozen people who held the reins at the company and knew the actual profit/loss figures and set strategic plans were talented, knowledgeable, exceptionally able people. Nevertheless, onetime chairman Walt Fallon spoke frustratedly about the need to "teach the elephant to dance," but always with the assumption that this would happen through the traditional "managerial mode" of strong centralization, a yoking of supermanager and supercomputer.

What was the problem? In the wake of the recession of 1981 and 1982, they desperately needed to understand what was holding the company back, slowing it down, adding to costs. Profits dropped from $1.1 billion in 1980 to $529 million in 1989. Fuji and the faltering national economy forced Eastman Kodak to find out.

The company did many things to learn to swim in the rough waters it found itself in. It took long, hard looks at every single dimension of the Eastman Kodak way of life. It looked at productivity, inventory turns, total cycle time, product quality. Kodak examined available options such as downsizing, restructurings, acquisitions, spinoffs, and mergers — even at an old idea with a new name, outsourcing. In a series of agonizing restructuring, Kodak let go almost 20,000 people, primarily through early retirements.

Eastman Kodak hired consultants by the planeload. It kept its own corporate ear to the ground to hear how other large companies were coping with change. A major step for the company was breaking itself into 17 units in 1982, with two massive manufacturing centers in the Rochester area: Kodak Park, where most of the sensitized film products were made, and Kodak Apparatus Division, where components and subsystems were made. Decentralizing Eastman Kodak, first structurally, and gradually as a matter of corporate climate, was a steady theme for the company from 1982 on.

But at Kodak demassification itself was the payoff on a long shot. It began with George Hannye, an Eastman Kodak career man who, over the course of 30 years with the company, had his finger in most of its pies — in marketing, information services, manufacturing, accounting, and international facilities. Hannye was a corporate troubleshooter, though some might say troublemaker. He was not a typical manager by any stretch, but the kind every great company cultivates a half dozen or so of — people who are quick studies, stubborn cusses who, once they are sure they are right about something, won't let anything, including the niceties of corporate politics, steer them off course.

DEMASS AT EASTMAN KODAK

In 1986 George Hannye returned to Rochester from an international assignment. He reported directly to Vice Chairman Phil Samper, who along with Chairman Colby Chandler and Chief Executive Officer Kay Whitmore, were the troika running Eastman Kodak.[2] Hannye was to function as if he were an external consultant. Any level of Kodak manager could "hire" him at no cost.

Hannye's reports went only to the managers hiring him and not to anyone in the troika. This arrangement permitted managers to speak candidly to him without fear of Hannye passing upward the "real story" or the "real numbers" to top management.

Frank Zaffino, who was in charge of Kodak's Apparatus Division (KAD), hired Hannye. It was a daunting assignment. KAD is a city unto itself, with its own marked freeway exit, one of the most massive centralized industrial installments anywhere in the world. It is Eastman Kodak's version of Henry Ford's Rouge Plant: everything happens there, from warehousing to design, engineering, manufacturing by over a hundred different processes, to packaging and shipping.

From front to back the KAD building is a 2.5-mile walk. If you come in from the east entrance you actually cross town lines, from Rochester to Ogden. A sign right in the middle of this massive structure reads, "Welcome to the town of Ogden." Calling by pay phone from the front end of the building to the rear is a toll call!

One of Hannye's first recommendations was to shut down KAD completely and start all over again from scratch. His reasoning was that the cost per square foot being allocated to each department was too much, much higher than comparable space available in western New York.

There was another problem, though — what to do with over 100 intertwined manufacturing departments? Many of the KAD departments were manufacturing very specialized components for multiple products. These same components could be sold to other companies for their products but Eastman Kodak didn't do that type of thing. Nevertheless, changes in the company's product mix resulted in many departments having excess capacity. They were all dressed up to produce, but there was nowhere to go.

You could dismantle the department and sell its assets, tool and die machines, mostly, and get a dime's return on the dollar, and leave empty, expensive space where the unit once stood. You could continue running the unit at a loss, even though you would have to bend over backwards to find uses for it. You could spin off the unit, wish it well, and charge the new owners rent — an awkward solution, to say the least. If you did shut it down, what did you do with the employees?

None of those solutions offered the kind of flexibility a manager requires in a business world where market conditions change direction faster than a ricocheting bullet. Hannye knew that shutting down KAD was not in the cards, certainly not in one fell swoop. But he decided that Kodak had to radically de-emphasize the kind of big-barn thinking KAD represented.

KAD had built its own Manufacturing Resources Planning (MRP II) computer software. In truth, KAD had totally rewritten a canned software package. On paper, software development had cost KAD over $50 million over the previous eight years, but costs were actually even higher than that. Any changes Hannye recommended would mean millions of dollars more in new costs. This was the offer he made to Zaffino: "You pick any department, and I will install a complete MRP II software package there in six months at a cost of $50,000. If you are not satisfied with the installation, you pay nothing — my budget will take the hit."

The six-month period, he stipulated, would begin the moment Hannye and his team decided which MRP II package to install. To give a hint as to Hannye's personality: he then went to Vice Chairman Phil Samper to get $50,000 added to his budget! After much internal discussion, Zaffino chose the target department: Eastman Kodak's Plastic Injection Molding facility. The unit, whose main job was creating plastic camera bodies, had good machinery, good people out on the shop floor, and strong management in a smart factory man named George Fellows. But Injection Molding appeared lost in terms of efficiency, turnaround, and economy. The real reason this department was picked was because George Fellows greatly distrusted computers! It was a good marriage, because, basically, so did Hannye.

"I didn't always hate mainframe computers," Hannye explained. "The name of the game today, though, is flexibility. If you can't rapidly change your operation to meet the many changes occurring in the marketplace, you're dead. No one — IBM included — claims mainframe applications are flexible or easily changed.

"Mainframes give you no advantages at all in return for the incredible disadvantages of inflexibility and high cost. A new release of any of our mainframe applications involved many thousands of hours of programmers' time. It was hard to tell after a while if it was working for you, or you were working for it. With this prejudice in mind," Hannye said, "I set out to select the best MRP II software for Plastic Injection Molding. I assumed it would be a program mounted on a small mini-mainframe system — and off we would go."

A surprise option asserts itself. Hannye had several bright people assisting him with data gathering and other chores, and one was Arthur Adriano. Adriano had helped Hannye design and install computer applications in Kodak's international distributing subsidiaries. He was now put in charge of obtaining bids, specs, and other input from the usual assortment of mini-mainframe manufacturing software providers. Since Hannye already had a pet package in mind, Adriano's evaluation project was to be just a cursory investigation.

However, word got out to the various manufacturing software providers, who sensed a windfall if they could get their product through the tiny door at Plastic Injection Molding and into the larger world of Eastman Kodak. As a result, Adriano was deluged with vendors' requests to be included in his research. One of the vendors was a microcomputer-based MRP II software package that Adriano tested and liked and convinced Hannye to select. Hannye respected Adriano's technical expertise, and he liked the videotaped training seminars that the software package came with.

Training was important to Hannye's plan. It meant that users could be trained while the new data base was being built. And it overcame one of the biggest hurdles Hannye was to face in demassifying any business unit — getting computer-wary workers and department managers to learn to use the new system.

Taking on the behemoth. It was at this point that Hannye and his team fully understood the radical departure they were on the brink of making. He and his band of demass commandos were preparing to assault Goliath, the behemoth of centralization and massive mainframe computing, armed with the equivalent of a slingshot — the lowly personal computer.

Fortunately, Hannye had a friend in high places. Phil Samper supported him and that meant a lot. But perhaps more important, Frank Zaffino, the new vice president and general manager of Eastman Kodak's Elmgrove plant, was coming to many of the same conclusions about massive-system-supported manufacturing as Hannye, though from another direction.

"We never set out to replace the largest systems with the smallest systems," said Zaffino. "All that was clear to me back in 1986 was that the current massive system didn't work and could not be made to work for the future. We knew that a distributive system made more sense for a whole variety of reasons. First of all, you could delegate ownership of the data base to the users. That is extremely meaningful because it means that, for the first time ever, your numbers will be accurate, and thus useful."

This last point was borne out by the experience at Plastic Injection Molding. Once the unit had created its own data base and compared it against data downloaded from the mainframe, the mainframe data proved to be startlingly inaccurate. Evidently, no one had previously been too concerned about feeding the "big system in the sky" accurate information.

"Second," Zaffino continued, "distributive systems allow you to look at departments more as self-contained units than before, when they were simply destinations at the bottom of the flowchart, at the end of the long line of mainframe information routing. And that 'self-contained' sense was very important to us. It meant all managers could be responsible for their own inventory, the accuracy of their data, for their costs. These are appealing characteristics."

It was Zaffino who actually coined the phrase "street of shops," envisioning the company as a megalopolis broken down into small, knowledgeable, intimate business teams of 100 people or so, each doing what it can do with pride, competence, efficiency, and profitability, just like a street of shops, with the corporation serving as traffic cop to the busy traffic.

Zaffino is intelligent, intense, and nondoctrinaire. "We're not wedded to the word demassification," he told me. "We're not even saying that the approach we took at KAD is the only way to go. All we're saying is that it works, that it works better than anything else we investigated, and that we are 100 percent committed to it."

Thus began Kodak's thrust toward demassification with the Apparatus Division's decision to transform its monolithic manufacturing operation into a "street of shops" — a clearly missioned assortment of unbureaucratic, self-managed business units, each given its own information-processing system and a clear set of business objectives to be achieved.

Another player at Eastman Kodak was Kathy Hudson. Coming aboard as vice president of Information Systems in 1988, and moving on in 1992, Hudson took the opportunity to send a warning-shot across the corporate bow when she took her 50-person Information Management Committee, which she was supposed to meet with annually to set a course for corporate computing, and reorganized it in a flash into a lean, mean 15-person squad. Hudson brought decisiveness and clarity to the process of demassifying, seeing the possibility for simulated decentralizing of business units with a maximum "biological limit" of about 200 people and a minimum of 40.

Hudson was an unusual combination of innovator and realist. In her tenure as vice president of Information Systems, it was her ability to see realities that escape other people, like the expense of large system maintenance, that fueled her talent for innovation. She was enough of a realist to know that no company would undertake change as drastic as demass unless it knew it was in trouble —"deep tapioca" was how she phrased it — and enough of an innovator to know that great challenges usually lead to great opportunities. "People don't do daring things unless they have to," she said.

Demassification is not always obvious, Hudson said. "We have data that suggests that a well-run mainframe system is potentially cheaper, in the long run, than a personal computer/local area network-based system. The problem is, they are not usually well run. The other problem is that expense is not our sole concern — flexibility, and the long-term gains in quality and true product-cost reduction, are far more important."

Crisis forces us to examine our possibilities from scratch. Managers thrive on crises; some even overdramatize them in order to galvanize and motivate their troops. Eastman Kodak, under the leadership of Zaffino and Hudson and the entrepreneurial spirit of George Hannye, was mobilizing for a fresh approach to manufacturing.

Although, according to Hannye, he and Zaffino seldom agreed on anything specifically, he could always rely on Zaffino to be there to back him up on his efforts to take sluggish departments and recast them as entrepreneurial "simulated businesses."

Hannye moved quickly to install a half-dozen personal computers in Plastic Injection Molding. He sat the first group of workers down at the PCs and showed them how the new system would restore local ownership within the organization.

Two of the six personal computers went out on the shop floor to track manufacturing and inventory processes. Several more were plugged in behind the glass-walled offices right on the plant floor, where in-company accounting, purchasing, planning, engineering, and design professionals could use them.

These were employees who moved from central air-conditioned offices onto the plant production floor. Yet the prevailing attitude among those moved was remarkably upbeat. Many workers mentioned to Hannye that the change was the best thing that had happened to them in years. The reason? For the first time, workers were being asked how to run their business instead of being told how to do it.

The workers were taught how to enter their own bills of material and to chart cycle time and inventory turns. It was surprisingly easy, and workers were delighted to have the chance to verify numbers on their own.

A slightly more daunting task was teaching workers who had been insulated from the dollars and cents aspect of their work that it was their responsibility to keep their craft above the red line. It was a major reorientation, for that meant they were no longer just designers, engineers, etc., they were *in business*, and team success required a higher level of care than their years of specialization and narrow job descriptions prepared them for.

On July 1, six individuals were picked to work on the installation of the new system. Five came from within Plastic Injection Molding. The progress this team made was phenomenal. By September the department was operational!

Kodak's "demassification czar." In this final task of immersing workers in the new, demassified workplace, Hannye had one additional ally. Jack Philbin was the sixth person picked by Frank Zaffino to join the installation team.

Philbin wasn't high up on the corporate totem pole, but he was probably the firmest believer in the productivity power of demass. An unusual combination of leader (he once had 300 planners working under him) and loner (taking on central administration at a *Fortune* 500 company is hardly a yes-man's assignment), Jack Philbin inherited the mantle of demassification czar at Kodak when George Hannye retired. A lifetime Eastman Kodak employee, Philbin worked at 27 jobs in 28 years with the company, having worked in engineering, camera manufacturing, payroll, accounting, systems (twice), production control, on up to his formal title as manager of distributed manufacturing support systems. Philbin, now retired, will be the first to tell you his real job was a strange combination of cheerleader/wheedler/cajoler.

Jack Philbin had the exhilarating idea that the magic of demass has nothing to do with the way people get information, and everything to do with what people do with the information once they have it. To him, demass began with the concept of worker empowerment. "Under demassification, information isn't dropped at whim from a bomb bay 20,000 feet overhead — it's right there, on site, three shifts a day. The personal computer approach frees individuals to ask questions, share ideas, get things done, quickly and flexibly."

Jack Philbin was a "go in and do it" sort, and still is. He and his teams took pride in being able to go in and fashion a business unit of 50 to 150 workers where before people only saw indistinct processes.

In the March 20, 1989 issue of *Industry Week*, Philbin said that there was no way to overemphasize the importance of employees "owning" their departmental data. "The synergism of people working together in a small business unit, within a large corporation, has improved employee morale, strengthened communications, and achieved large cost savings."

Why demassification worked at Kodak. The experiment at Plastic Injection Molding was a success almost from the start. "We are basically a $25 million business, with about 250 people, 100 molding machines, and an engineering staff," said manager George Fellows. "Five years ago we were part of a centralized system. The computer used to shoot us a big slew of paper, with no rhyme or reason, and certainly no resemblance to what we knew was happening. It was a totally 'seat of the pants' operation in those days.

"With the smaller computers, we had the chance to redo all that data," Fellows said. "We absolutely refused to download the junk the big computer had in its bowels. It took weeks to enter by hand the data we knew to be actual, but we did it. And as soon as we had done that, we got control of our business. Hannye and his people promised we would be in charge, and except for financial operations, we were. We don't operate as a profit center but as a cost center, but the philosophy here is that of a profit center. Our goal is to operate at zero profit, but I'd much rather be on the profit side by a couple bucks than be in the red.

"It's been a total turnaround for us. Five years ago business was heading out one door and we were heading out the window. Now we're recovered and thriving."

Hannye won his bet with Frank Zaffino, finishing in less than six months and coming in under $50,000. Plastic Injection Molding was the first to make the crossing from dependence to independence, but it was not the last. About 100 units at Eastman Kodak have since been transformed, with more lining up. That usually means yanking the plug on the mainframe terminals, training people to use new, more compact hardware, telling them to verify their own data (not simply download existing, inaccurate data from the company mainframes), and educating them on what it means to be a business — what profit means, what accountability means, what metrics to use to measure success and failure on the shop floor, what just-in-time means, where and how quality comes into the picture.

Of all the hundred-odd conversions, only one ran into obstacles it could not overcome and had to revert to the previous system. As for all the rest, managers are flushed with pride that the numbers on the walls are *their* numbers and that they're accurate. Engineers, designers, purchasing agents, and accountants work alongside shop supervisors, each one dedicated to success for the business unit. Banners fly from the factory beams: *Quality Is Everywhere. JIT Beats "Just In Case."*

And not far away, at one of a half-dozen central computer rooms at KAD, the old machines sit blinking, unattended. Where once 70 software attendants ministered to mainframes, quiet darkness now reigns.

Walking the tightrope. Demassification of manufacturing at Eastman Kodak has continued apace since that first success of George Hannye and George Fellows at Plastic Injection Molding. Before taking early retirement in 1991, Jack Philbin walked a tightrope. On the one hand, he wanted to spread the word that demass works. On the other, he didn't want to scare people who were honestly committed to existing structures, or who pictured demass as the manufacturing equivalent of a mob of angry villagers with torches.

But his conviction and pride in the process were evident when he escorted visitors through KAD. Every month they came, with spiral notepads, tape recorders, and video cameras, eager to learn what they could about how one of the largest and most conservative of the great U.S. manufacturing companies was learning the swing step.

Walter Goddard, president of Oliver Wight Companies, a well-known MRP II consulting firm, is a believer in Eastman Kodak's demass program. "To Kodak's credit, they are getting MRP II next to the user and having him accept responsibility for using it properly," he observed.

Today, Kodak can point to many signs of success: about 100 demassified manufacturing units worldwide, including businesses in India, Mexico, Japan, Ireland, Australia, and England; the quality banners draped from the factory beams; the production reports taped to every door and panel showing each department how it is doing with its goals, based upon its own data; the alert look on workers' faces as they go about the business they understand best and are accountable for.

Philbin isn't hung up on externals or language. He doesn't care what you call what he did — demass, employee involvement, participatory management. "Demassification is just one face of the overall move we are seeing toward flow manufacturing," Philbin said. "Deep down, this shift is not dependent upon MRP II or other software or computers. It's about empowerment, about moving out of the old paradigm of control and into a new paradigm of trust.

"Demass to me means transforming the way people think about the work they do, so that it matters in a very real way to them. This process, of transforming a cost center into a profit center, is incredibly powerful, and it is all part and parcel of total quality management. The way I see it, you can't do total quality management without employee involvement. And demassification is the surest way I know to put the power where the action is, with the people who do the work."

Empty warehouses. The most visual result of all this may be the transformation of three huge, previously highly automated warehouses that circle the massive factory city. When

Philbin first came on the job they were the pride of Eastman Kodak, after the mainframes the most visible symbol of the centralized philosophy of the company's grand old days.

As we motored by, some nine months before his retirement in late 1991, Jack Philbin pointed out the three immense automated warehouses, built when the company was still certain that massification in inventory and in production was the right way to go.

"See those three big barns?" he said. "Empty, empty, and about a third full. There are lots of people around here who believe there's something very wasteful about that. I don't. Automated warehouse managers may do inspired things to make their automated warehouses more efficient," Philbin said, but no automated warehouse manager comes up with an idea to make his automated warehouse unnecessary.

Today, Eastman Kodak's automated warehouses are nearly irrelevant. The "real" inventory is kept on hand within their respective businesses, in small, fast-moving amounts. A waste of good money, these vast, empty, high-tech barns? In a sense, maybe, but not really. Philbin knows the real numbers on keeping massive warehouses full, and they are not good. "I think about those empty buildings," Philbin said, characteristically tucking his shirttail in while hitching up his trousers, "and I smile."

And while warehouse managers can keep pushing technology to make their automated warehouses the best in the business, the fact is that there probably shouldn't be that much inventory; there shouldn't be automated warehouses. Yes, they do a fantastic job of inventory management. But it's a job that shouldn't have to be done. Just by being there, blocking out the sky, they are saying to the unsuspecting company, "Feed me. Fill me. Use me."

THE FUTURE OF DEMASSIFICATION AT KODAK

With Philbin's retirement, it is unclear whether anyone at Eastman Kodak will assume the lead role for advocacy of demassification. Finding a spokesperson who can instill the same degree of evangelical fervor that Philbin did is a hard enough task. But before it does that, the company must ask itself if it wants to continue down the path of employee empowerment via demassification.

Hannye and Philbin are gone. Hannye, who some day will be revered far and wide as a pioneer in demass and the scourge of top-heavy management, quietly retired to Tennessee. Philbin, the cheerleader and articulator for the "street-of-shops" empowerment process that Hannye launched, is now a consultant, spreading the gospel of employee empowerment and information-processing technology downsizing to other big companies.

Within the corridors of Eastman Kodak the signs of backsliding are apparent. In the face of complaints that information passage to top management was too slow and that corporate reports were coming out intolerably late, central MIS started to react. Central MIS's reaction can be viewed as a move to more comfortable ground:

- to spending more time planning how to someday tie everything together electronically (central control)
- to spending less time equipping independent business units with data processing tools that they need today (empowerment)
- to funneling more money into developing new computing systems' interoperability standards (central control)

- to spending less money equipping individual business units with departmental-level systems (empowerment)

Information services may decide to invite large centralized systems back in to get everything back under comfortable control! Eastman Kodak is at that awkward moment when the pain and turmoil of transition is dimming the vision of what empowerment is bringing. But central control and local empowerment are inherently unreconcilable. Kodak can't have it both ways; no large company can.

Eastman Kodak, like so many American companies, is facing a decade of remarkable challenge. Just as Fuji challenged Kodak's supremacy in film making in the 1980s, so now a new wave of technology, digital image processing, threatens to upset the technology of chemical image processing, in which Kodak is the world leader. Industry analysts describe this latest challenge as having "life-or-death" dimensions for Kodak because it encompasses corporate strategy, technology, marketing, and distribution.

Now, more than ever, Kodak needs the best from each employee. By definition this must be a voluntary contribution. The emotional source of this voluntary contribution is empowerment.

Eastman Kodak is a great company, a national treasure. It has achieved remarkable progress in empowering workers closest to the action to become actual businesspeople. This is what Kodak's "street of shops" has been about from the very first.

I sincerely hope the advocates of demassification tenaciously persevere and continue moving Kodak toward total worker empowerment. It's important to Eastman Kodak. It's important to all American business.

6
How To Do It

Where to start? How to measure? Who manages? These are the practical questions chief executive officers have about the process of demassification. There is no single, one-size-fits-all method for demassifying a large company. Most companies that are demassifying are doing it one toe in the water at a time.

Want to see a CEO's temperature rise? Say that the company's operational problems are being caused by "poor internal communications." Poor communications is such a clichéd diagnosis today — so vague, so broad, and so seemingly inescapable — that it leads to much high-level hair-pulling.

Sometimes we think we are communicating but the message isn't getting through, and the consequences are grievous. In business, the biggest problems usually boil down to poor communication, and that's precisely where demass can help most. But the question remains: How does a company go about implementing a demass strategy?

There is no cookie-cutter implementation pattern all companies can follow. Large companies that are successful without radical decentralization will not want to redo their entire corporate apparatus. But they may want to target individual business units that have been having noticeable problems in quality, information handling, and process flow for "test-bed demassification."

Companies functioning in a highly centralized fashion, regardless of whether they have been decentralized into divisions, are in a position to mandate demassification throughout the company, throughout all divisions, throughout a single division, or in strategically selected business units. Companies that are essentially confederacies — families of companies, holding companies of autonomous divisions, or corporate conglomerates — will probably encounter demassification as a process that trickles up from the division level.

Demassification can be spearheaded by an individual either within the corporation or outside it. His or her role should be that of a consultant to top management. While being given broad latitude in sidestepping the usual corporate bureaucracy, this person must also be given clear authority to make waves and to spend company money. This individual will be your demass director (or czar or advocate).

Earlier, we used the title "demassification czar," but that probably isn't the best description of what a demass director is. Kodak's Jack Philbin laughs at the idea that he was ever a czar of anything. "Czars don't work that hard," he laughed. "I guess I was like a czar in that my work was cross-functional. I could not rely on a specific body of specialized knowledge. I had to be all over the place, dealing with and understanding all kinds of people. And, like a czar, I had the power to cut a bit of red tape at times. But 'demassification czar' is a contradiction in terms. Demass is the distribution of power, not the solitary flexing of it."

The demass director may not have the power to order the restructuring of a unit. But he or she should have the authority to:

- meet with troubled business units and discuss ways in which power and information can be controlled locally, at the lowest possible level;
- suggest ways in which units can be broken down into even smaller operational subunits;
- make critical decisions on implementation, scheduling, and training for the entity to be demassified.

The demass fast-track. According to Philbin, one of the points of greatest resistance is that demassifying will involve a lengthy and frustrating period of adaptation, training, and pain. This is because department-level managers are accustomed to the time and effort it took to do anything new using a mainframe or minicomputer.

"It's not necessarily so," Philbin says. "It can be, but it doesn't have to be. In the early days, I was set up as a consultant, accountable to the office of the president. That was an important credential; it meant I wasn't just some guy spouting off. There was a corporate goal — greater flexibility, quicker inventory turns, faster new product rollout. I wasn't the cure-all to the company's problems, I was just one guy, taking one approach. This can be a very unpopular job. Some people, noticeably in information services, just grit their teeth when they hear my name. But I wasn't a loose cannon. I had a plan that the company was aware of and supported, at the very highest levels."

Overcoming inertia. One of the biggest problems with creating a "street-of-shops" structure will be getting the bureaucracy to budge. The system you are trying to change does not want to change. Stopping the current flow is roughly equivalent to tackling Godzilla. There is a tremendous amount of resistance. Getting the system to move in the opposite direction requires the application of great force.

Distributing corporate information services personnel into operational organizations and downsizing corporate computers to more flexible and less expensive networks of personal computers and workstations normally accompanies organizational demassification. Here are five classic reasons CEOs are given, usually by heads of information services, for going slowly or indefinitely delaying the actual decision to proceed on downsizing their corporate computer systems:

- "We are so tied up trying to make the current system work, we can't even think about doing something radically different."
- "Our internal requirements are so unique that we simply must design and build — or at the very least, significantly customize — the software we deploy."
- "Our 15-year-old corporate software is so full of patches we don't dare switch. The only people who really understood it quit over five years ago!"
- "All large plants must run on mainframes, mid-sized plants on minis, and small plants on networked personal computers — maybe!"
- "We're already committed to the hardware platform we want to standardize on, companywide. So now we simply must limit ourselves to compatible hardware and software that will run on it."

The CEO who is prepared recognizes that change is equally disturbing to all managers, high-tech, low-tech, and no-tech. It may help to think of corporate inertia as ordinary constipation. You know that prunes will alleviate the situation. But are six too many? Are three enough? Jack Philbin's experiences at Eastman Kodak seemed to indicate that it's better, just this one time, to be sorry than safe: eat the boxful of prunes and clear the area. Lesser efforts are halfhearted efforts. To get to your destination, you may have to overshoot a little.

George Hannye believes that at one time major corporations needed to develop their own software, but that time has passed. "Today, external vendors' software is superior to anything a corporation can build on its own. It is built to satisfy the needs of many companies, which means flexibility to change is built in."

THE TASK OF THE CEO

CEOs will want to know what role to play in demassifying a business unit. My advice is to be a doting orchestrator— a blender, weigher, listener, and decider — but keep a low profile. A division cannot radically decentralize with the CEO looking over its shoulder. Remember that the business-unit personnel are experts at what they do, or they should be.

In a demassified system CEOs play a role different from that in a centralized or merely decentralized organization. In centralized companies CEOs are seen as supermanagers, primary decision makers, killers of giants, and untiers of knots. They are like perfectly tuned pianos. They personally "tune" their immediate subordinates, who in turn tune their subordinates, and so on down the line. The problem is that after all this sequential tuning no two pianos are quite in tune. And centralized CEOs wonder why the corporate music sounds so discordant.

In demassified companies, CEOs have a different role. They help establish and communicate the mission for the organization, set business goals and objectives, affirm the guidelines by which people will work to achieve those objectives, set limits on what resources are allocated, and work day after day to keep people on track. These CEOs also must make the unpleasant decisions sometimes required when a business unit can no longer contribute positively to the bottom line. The CEO of a demassified company serves as a central tuning fork against which every piano is tuned.

Demassified CEOs are recruiters, hirers, and trainers. This is not to say they must do these things alone. But they must take an interest in these dimensions to a new degree. For it is not wise to empower bad or inept or ignorant people. Empowerment only works with people who understand the goals of the company, and their own jobs.

Demass is not a perfect system. CEOs never have the resources to do exactly what they'd like — they have to make do with the 88 piano keys they have. But a talented CEO will bring the company back into harmony. And once you have harmony, the chances for a good melody — motivated people working together toward agreed-upon goals — rise dramatically.

Define, qualify, empower and equip. These are the elemental tasks of the demassifying company manager: define goals, hire qualified people, and continually train them. Empower them to use their individual talents to achieve corporate goals, and equip them with suitable tools to do the work at hand.

Inadvertent demassification. The technology downsizing activity of demassification is not always part of a grand strategy. Sometimes it happens unintentionally. A struggling business unit will become fed up with mainframe delays and downtime; to get around centralized bottlenecks it will install its own networked system. Sometimes it happens when a faraway business unit, such as an international operation, grows impatient with its lethargic umbilical-cord system, and starts casting about for something more flexible, faster, and less expensive.

With their own performance data at their fingertips, workers rise to a higher level of involvement and productivity, and exude an unmistakable air of empowerment and entrepreneurship. Suddenly, without intending to demassify, the business unit has the early earmarks of a stand-alone company, and all because the unit took it upon itself to rearrange some furniture.

You can demassify without having heard the word. Much of Tom Peters's advice to corporations hinges on organizationally stripping away layers of bureaucracy and empowering workers with proper tools — the two strands of the demassification rope. Peters's February 11, 1992 article in the *New York Times* offered the following "must-do" tasks that are a facsimile of the key tenets of demassification:

- Reorganize into independent business units of 250 or fewer people.
- Redeploy one-third of all staff members at the division level or above to customer-focused operations. Within five years reduce headquarters staff to a maximum of 10 people per billion dollars in revenue.
- Require remaining members of centralized staffs to "sell their services" to line units at market rates. Meanwhile, allow line units to buy at any time, from anybody, anywhere.[1]

How far to demassify? Ideally, the size of the team or independent business unit size should be as small as possible

— about 50 to 250 people. I know of one instance where the business unit consisted of lots of equipment, but only 10 employees.

Some firms feel a business unit should be staffed up to a size of about 500 people. Under normal circumstances, more than 500 people simply cannot learn to think and react as a team — too many people will feel uninvolved. The smaller the group, the greater the sense of participant ownership.

One CEO goal should be directing the reorganization of monolithic manufacturing down into manageable business units. Make sure that what you want to attempt is operationally practical. The units you want to recast must have manageable bureaucratic hurdles to vault over.

Clear the way for demass. Eliminate top-down, imprecise corporate allocations, such as information services, central purchasing, warehouse allocations, and central accounting — the really big offenders.

When your people choose a computer and software for the demassified units, push for reasonable standardization. Initially, all that will be important is that your teams talk to one another. Independent business units, departments, and divisions need to put their heads together and share data. They need to be connected electronically. When communicating, it helps if they are not trying to share data using a dozen different unconnectable systems. Demass breaks a company into many villages, but all should speak compatible languages, as well as communicate by phone.

Demass is as much about information as it is about organization, and this information must flow freely throughout the implementation process. Success and improvement require that feedback loops be instituted at every "seam" in every process. Employees must communicate with one another to find problems, identify them, and correct them.

With their own information at their disposal, with encouragement, and with their success linked to the company's bottom line, that is exactly what they will do.

HOW TO LAUNCH DEMASSIFICATION IN YOUR COMPANY

The easy thing to say about the right way to begin demassifying is "It all depends." And, well, yes, it does depend.

How you demassify depends on a host of factors: what kind of company you are; *your* size, number of products or product lines; geographic spread of locations; the number, size, and distribution of your customers and suppliers; your company's cultural heritage; levels of management; and your management team's capabilities and biases.

How you demassify depends on *why* you have decided to demassify the company, *what* you want to gain, *how* you want to do it and over *what time frame*, and *how much* of your time and mindshare you intend to dedicate to the effort. It depends on how much power you have, and how you plan to expend it or conserve it.

I usually assume that a company's decision to radically decentralize organizationally — to downsize information-processing systems capabilities to become operational tools of independent business units — is mandated by outside forces such as competition that may be rapidly overtaking, or has already overtaken, the company.

Demassification cannot take place overnight. In fact, if you are a huge corporation, and you attempt to demassify one unit at a time, it may take more than five years, a span exceeding most CEOs' strategic plans, not to mention their tenures. The corporation must make reorganization of its many operations an ongoing commitment. A one-at-a-time pace suggests less than total commitment. The most sensible approach is to try pilot units, learn quickly the lessons that must be learned, work out the bugs, and then move on to an entire division. My best sense is that a giant company can be changed organizationally in as little as three years. Changing the company's culture, the piled-up proclivities and resentments that are its operating personality, may take longer.

As CEO, you may be an astute and gifted leader, but you probably are like most people in one respect: you would just as soon avoid change. But if you are going to make demassification work for your company, then change you must. Even more daunting will be the challenge of getting your whole chain of command to change along with you. Leading a massive multinational corporation into demassification is a role the CEO cannot delegate to anyone else.

The situation. To illustrate how demassification can be launched, let's create a hypothetical situation. Remember Pete Bates from Chapter 1, the harried CEO of the nation's 82nd largest manufacturing corporation? Let's use his company as our example. Pete's company is about a $6 billion concern. It develops, manufactures and, through a variety of sales channels, markets electronic products for both consumers and businesses. Half of sales are domestic, half are international.

The company is already decentralized into 15 operating divisions with $100 million to $1 billion in sales each. Each division is more or less autonomous with its own research and development, production facilities, and sales force. Numerous centralized staff services are located at corporate headquarters. Among these are human resources, accounting, purchasing, order processing, payroll, warehousing, and of course, information systems.

Each of these central corporate services is more or less replicated within each division level with straight-line reporting to the division president and dotted-line reporting to the respective corporate services vice president. Also there are highly automated corporate warehouses along with smaller division warehouses. Each division is allocated expenses based on measured usage.

The CEO (Pete), along with his president and chief financial officer, are supported by a relatively lean headquarters staff. Pete has good rapport with and confidence in his president and chief financial officer. Five of the company's division presidents are strong performers, rising stars with solid track records, although their numbers for these past few years have been marginal. Seven division presidents are above-average performers but, based on this year's numbers, their jobs are on the line. And the final three division presidents are on the ropes because they have been marginal performers at best.

Revenue growth is spotty across the divisions and miserable overall at the enterprise level. There have been too many manufacturing problems with new product lines, and competition is reportedly gaining market share across the board. Expenses are growing faster than revenue; debt and interest burden are mounting; and return on shareholder equity has declined for the last three years. The stock price recently plummeted, following a stock analyst report that the company is asset heavy, people laden, and bureaucracy ridden. Pete is liked and respected for what he has accomplished in the past. But Board members are muttering that the promised and long-awaited turnaround is overdue.

Two previous employee-reduction programs succeeded only in making most employees mad; they did nothing to improve margins. Now, employees are starting to talk about unionizing!

Given this set of circumstances, Pete has decided his core problem is that the company still hasn't found the right way to motivate employees to become more productive. Following lengthy soul searching and a lot of talking to fellow executives in the industry, he has decided to demassify his company. Sold the Board on it, too. He told them he wants to regain the entrepreneurial attitude that was in place when he was climbing the corporate ladder. They bought it — even got a little excited for a change. But they're not noted for patience.

So, what should Pete do?

A CEO-driven strategy to demassify. The most important element of the strategy to demassify must be that it's conceived and driven by the CEO alone. Developed and refined with advice and counsel, yes, but the CEO must structure and pace the plan. The driving force behind the plan must be the CEO.

Let's assume Pete is such a CEO and that he asked me to advise him. He is not asking me to help sell his Board on demass; he's already done that. He is asking me how to get started and structure an enterprise-wide, overall strategy for demassification.

First I would ask Pete where he felt the rough spots would be, including both personnel and nonpersonnel situations. Pete and I would both understand that problems will continually surface as the company moves toward demassification, but focusing on problem identification up-front is the right place to start. Next, I would discuss with him the importance of moving successfully through seven measured steps. The steps are these:

1. Gain the support of your inner circle of executives.

2. Research and determine the extent to which your performance measurements system must be changed to accommodate the planned new organizational structure.
3. Do some high-level goal setting for line operations and staff services organizations.
4. Exhort your staff services executives to action.
5. Exhort your line operations executives to action.
6. Change the current thinking and direction of central information services management.
7. Communicate the demassification strategy to all employees.

Now let's look at each step in greater detail.

Step 1. Gain the support of your inner circle of executives. Share with your inner circle of direct reports what you see as the company's root problems, and then explain that demassification is the process that you support as a strategic solution.

Explain that demass is about employee empowerment at the independent business-unit level, not a headcount reduction program. Tell them that as a necessary part of this empowerment process, the company must emphasize downsizing its computer systems into business-unit-sized systems. These downsized systems are to be integral tools used by each business unit to improve business-unit productivity of people and assets.

Information connectivity will be more important than ever, but the company's new information-processing theme will be information availability, not information transmission.

Upward flow of information will be constrained to a minimum. The new rule: more summary information, much less detail. Horizontal flow of information will be emphasized.

Availability of information within the business unit will be maximized.

Problem identification will be the province of the independent business unit, not central staff's. Business units are to own and act upon the information for which they are responsible. They are to identify and address problems *as they occur*, not as a reaction resulting from problem identification done somewhere "higher up."

The idea is threefold: to maximize the operational autonomy of employee work teams closest to the customer action; to minimize reliance on or interference from corporate and division-level staff support operations; and to eliminate "allocations" to the greatest extent possible. Business units are to be equipped with the responsibility, authority, and tools necessary to directly control their group's productivity. They will be given business-unit-level goals and will be measured and held responsible for results achieved.

Explain in general terms the new "look and feel" of the goals. Explain how today's goals will be different from tomorrow's: continuously lowering break-even points; profitability per dollar invested and per headcount; continuous improvement versus benchmarked "best competitors" — all at the business-unit level. In many cases the new rules of the road will be that business-unit performance must surpass certain hurdle rates or that business unit will be shut down, re-missioned, or sold.

If a business unit's product or service can be strategically replaced by an external source, that business unit must, within a specific grace period, be performing at a level of performance superior to the competition.

In other words, the corporation will hereafter be removing the fat at a business-unit level. No longer will the division or the entire company try to cut headcount or expense budgets at some fixed rate across the whole organization — a process that necessarily removes muscle along with fat.

This will be a long session (or series of meetings), with a lot of give and take. You may want to bring in an outside specialist to help. The bottom-line goals of step 1 are for your inner circle to understand that you are committed to a demassification strategy and to gain their active support.

The word will quickly spread through the management hierarchy that change is coming and that you, the CEO, are the one pushing it. The education process will have begun. People had better get on the train, or get off the track!

Step 2. Research and determine how much your performance measurements system must be changed. Have your CFO create and chair a high-powered task force of fewer than 10 professionals to study the impact demassification will have on your current measurement system. Have your audit firm represented in the group.

This task force should discuss the following questions:

- Which of today's performance measurements are absolutely necessary?
- Why are they necessary?
- Who gets them?
- Who needs them to do his or her job?
- Which measurements are for internal management purposes?
- Which are for use with external reviewers or auditors?
- How will business-unit managers be budgeted and measured?
- How will new performance measurements roll up?
- How seamless will the transition from old measurements to new measurements be?

The task force must understand that financial and performance measurement emphasis is on detail at the business-unit level, less detail at the division level, and minimal detail at the enterprise level.

Step 3. Do some high-level goal setting. Create a small executive work team cochaired by the president and your best staff services executive (probably the one you are planning to move over to line management). Some sharp number-cruncher types will be needed. You should attend most of the meetings. These questions should be addressed early in the process by this work team:

- To what minimum level can the "office of the top executives" (i.e., the CEO, president, CFO and their immediate staffs) be reduced? The image of leanness presented here will influence all others.
- What is the purpose of each corporate-level staff services organization?
- Which staff services can be performed better at the operating division level?
- Which of these staff services should be done at a lower level, perhaps even at the independent business-unit level?

At whatever levels all staff services operations eventually operate, all must provide their services at what line operations considers competitive rates. Each will be given a specific grace period to make the transition to a competitive organizational structure.

Staff services' first duty will be to support the operating divisions, rather than upper management, and they will perform their mission at competitive rates and with competitive levels of customer-oriented service. Each staff service operation is to charge fees, not allocate costs, and it is to run a break-even operation.

All staff services operations identified as "untouchable" are to be so designated by the CEO. The eventual goal is to eliminate this kind of staff organization.

This work team should also pin down, to the degree possible, all allocation systems at work in the company today. The following questions can help guide these determinations:

- Who allocates to whom? How much is being allocated? Rank allocation categories by dollar size.
- Which allocations can be eliminated completely, and how soon?
- Which allocations will continue to be necessary, and why?
- Which interoperating division allocations can be eliminated?
- Which charges being allocated to manufacturing operations and that show up in product cost can be eliminated?

For line operations, set targets for the profitability level that each of the 15 operating divisions needs to reach within three years. The rationale for the profitability goals must be clearly defined. No divination by dart-throws!

Many companies use different versions of this "portfolio" approach. The portfolio approach involves asking what is to be invested in each business, and how much return is expected, based on available markets, product life cycles, and other criteria that vary significantly by type of company.

Important questions with the portfolio approach:

- Which businesses should be invested in? Which should be tasked to provide profits and positive cash flow? Over what time frames?

- After all the contributions are totaled, is overall performance satisfactory?
- How different are these business goals on a division-by-division basis than those currently in place?
- How much of the impact is coming from the change in how allocations are going to be handled in the future?

Step 4. Exhort your staff services executives to action. Call in the corporate staff vice presidents (human resources, accounting, information services, etc.) along with the president and chief financial officer. Share the company's overall performance problems. Depict the role you feel allocations play in those problems. Get their views. Show them the new allocations statistics put together by the executive work team. Discuss your vision for corporatewide demassification. Then describe in general terms their revised missions, why the change is necessary, how long they will have to make the changeover, and what they have to gain from this restructuring.

Now that you have their attention, explain that just as line divisions must become profitable businesses, so must they. Divisions may or may not use their services. They may have to reassign some of their personnel to the divisions. Ask them to study their own situations and complete a competitive analysis on alternative external services that divisions might use.

Step 5. Exhort your line operations executives to action. Meet with the 15 division presidents along with the president and chief financial officer. No one else, including staff members, should attend.

Discuss the company's overall problems, each division's contribution to these problems, and why you think that demassifying divisions into empowered individual business units is the process the company needs to implement.

Explain each division's new profitability goals, how they were determined, and why things must change, and quickly, or "none of us will be around to fix anything."

Tell them you would like to work with them on implementing demassification within their divisions to improve performance. Ask them to tell you how you can help. But if they are committed to meeting their goals some other way, that's their prerogative.

Tell them elimination of most allocations is a key element of the demassification strategy. (They should love that.) Show them the allocations statistics and analysis. Explain that after the agreed-on grace period, they are free to use internal staff services, or go outside. It is their decision. But urge them not to act too hastily, since some staff services may even be moved outward into the divisions.

Discuss the requirement for downsizing information-processing systems. Explain that you believe that it's necessary (and only fair) for local business units to see their performance numbers before management levels find out.

Business units should have the chance to solve their own problems themselves before being told to do it. Tell them, however, that you will be discussing with information services ways to best achieve this without creating technological chaos.

Review with them the need to break down their operating divisions into logical and properly sized independent business units. Tell them the maximum headcount is 250 people. Tell them they must establish business-unit-specific performance goals across their entire division. Let them know you understand that this won't be easy.

Discuss the criteria for what makes an independent business unit "independent." Tell them where they can get some help in identifying and defining these businesses-within-a-business. A tool-and-die shop in a fabricating plant can be easily circled and defined. Other businesses are less clearly defined. In any case, convince them that identifying and sizing independent business units is their job, and not to be shunted off to their subordinates.

Finally, indicate that while all 15 division presidents should get started as soon as possible, it is important to proceed in an orderly fashion. Ask all 15 to review the information received at this meeting and the company strategy for demassification, with their direct reports, and then get back to you with an indication of how quickly they will be prepared to start implementation. Let them know that you feel it would be best if three or fewer divisions implemented initially. Then, using the experience gained, proceed to implement demass across the company.

Possibly one of the largest division heads, who runs a giant manufacturing facility, will ask, “How in the world do you expect me to do this? My plate already overflows with things to do!” Explain that this is the corporate strategy to improve performance. You are giving them the option as division presidents not to participate in demassification. Their numbers, however, must improve — and quickly. That part is not an option.

Suggest that they should start with manufacturing operations. The concept is to break manufacturing down into a “street-of-shops” organization, with each department functioning as an independent business unit. These business units will each have responsibility for either a product line or a manufacturing process or a service. Business units must have crystal-clear customer focus and product focus.

Most business units, especially manufacturing business units, are to get off the shared mainframe system as soon as practical. To be truly independent, the business unit should run its own decision support information-processing system. Their data must be accurate, timely, and dependable. The software they use should be flexible so that it is adaptable to meet changing needs. Manufacturing departments will need an MRP II system.

Most MRP II software packages that run on networked personal computers can handle up to 100 multiple, interconnected user stations. Thus hardware investment can be matched to the department size. We shouldn't be hunting mosquitoes with an elephant gun.

Will the software force you to change the way you do business? Only if it is for the better. The main thing is that it will force you to think about the way you do business, and to ask questions about why you currently are doing business the way you are.

Work with corporate information services to select the software package that works best. This process should take no more than three months. The best canned packages are installable in six months or less. Success will come from business units embracing the strengths and manufacturing disciplines of the packages selected, and not from each unit trying to jerry-rig the software to accommodate exception-driven and probably outdated manufacturing practices. Don't let each business unit try to change the package; have them change their outdated business practices.

Plan to transition current funding from big mainframes to microcomputers. This transition should be accomplished without increasing overall computing expenditures.

Each business unit is to be assigned a profit target, even if it's a break-even target for a service unit. Each business unit should, for example, determine its break-even revenue level, then reduce this threshold by no less than 25 percent every 12 months. Specific performance goals are to be set as appropriate.

If an independent business unit does not have a skilled financial individual, one should be assigned. This financial person should be located near the plant floor. This person should stay continually aware of what allocations are being received from corporate; from the division; and from anywhere else in the company. One ultimate company goal should be to eliminate all allocations.

Step 6. Change the current thinking and direction of central information services management. It's time to call back the information systems vice president for a one-on-one meeting. Explain that the role of information services vice president is vital to the companywide success of demassification. Say that you want computers to be used in the company as operating tools within line operations — not as repositories of information for staff executives to peruse. You want to retain division and corporatewide control and auditability. But the emphasis must be on the business units autonomously using systems to run their businesses.

You don't want incompatible computers and software to proliferate like bunny rabbits across all divisions. By the same token, you don't want computer and software selections to be made top-down strictly for "standards and compatibility" reasons. The emphasis is to be on personal systems used intimately by individuals — personal information-processing systems used as tools to help them do their jobs.

You want to retain central information systems, but you want it to be a lot smaller and you want the mission changed. You want information services to get out of the software development and maintenance business and to focus on helping business units select the best packaged software to get their jobs done. Indicate that, to the extent possible, you'd like to eliminate mainframe computers; they should not be needed at a corporate level. In some companies this may not be possible, but in most it should be. There are alternatives, however. Some major companies rent time on university supercomputers when they need work done such as research number crunching.

Instruct the vice president of information services to educate everyone in the information-services department that time is money. An average decision implemented today is worth more than most great decisions implemented months from now.

Information services personnel are to continue conducting thorough analyses of competitive hardware and software, but they must also help divisions and business units make selection decisions quickly, understanding that packaged software and smaller computers are disposable. Tell them technology is moving so fast that flexibility must be considered more important than trying to implement rigid standards.

Ask this vice president which "consolidated" information-processing activities should be continued at the divisional or corporate levels, and which shouldn't. In most cases, these activities can be performed on powerful personal computers.

You and the chief financial officer will want continued corporate financial consolidations, but in a revised, less detailed format. The goal is to limit the amount of detail in corporate consolidations, not maximize it.

Finally, the information systems vice president is to understand that the information services headcount and budget are going to be significantly reduced because computing is being moved out to line operations. The job is going to become more difficult since the reduced staff must now assist business units in making good selection decisions and successful implementations.

Information services must begin coordinating appropriate product training programs for systems users as well as systems maintenance liaisons between users and the various hardware and software providers. They are to spend much less time with outside hardware vendors and far more time with internal business-unit people. Instead of drafting companywide information systems plans, information services should devote itself to ensuring that individual business units meet their productivity objectives.

Step 7. Communicate the demassification strategy to all employees. When the buzz within the company has reached the right level of intensity, issue a notice to all employees indicating what is to be done and why. As soon as possible, broadcast to all employees your strategy and goals.

Ask each of the 3 operating division presidents who will be demassifying (ahead of the other 12 divisions) to explain what they're doing and how it's going. Hold lower level communication meetings and inspire enthusiasm in all the employees of these three divisions. Make them feel special. Create an atmosphere where those employees who are not in demassifying divisions are eager to get started.

IS YOUR COMPANY DEMASS-ABLE?

The previous "how-to" scenario and associated advice is necessarily sketchy; it leaves out a ton of important details. It also omits the very real question: "How do I keep my company, once it's in motion toward demass, from backsliding to autocratic central controls?"

Nothing is certain in business or in life. If a coup could threaten perestroika in Gorbachev's Soviet Union, it is certainly possible for some anxious managers to re-seize the reins of organizations they believe are running amok. But, as with the coup against Gorbachev, such an effort is likely to fail, because it doesn't address the underlying issues of organizational success.

Eastman Kodak itself, my best example of a company trying to reform itself from a slow-moving mass into a flexible "street of shops," appears to be rethinking the bold course it has pioneered.

Can the toothpaste of empowerment be squeezed somehow back into the tube? It may be possible. Will the company then be able to compete with more flexible competitors? No.

Depending on your situation, you will have to consider whether a corporate-level demass director should be named or if each division should have a separate demass director heading a small implementation team.

Still another question only the CEO can answer is: When I demassify, what do I keep and what do I throw away or farm out? You know right now where your company's most effective talents lie. Chances are that you are leveraging those talents right now, but not as effectively as you might if you took an extra-hard look at your operations.

I wonder, for instance, whether Kodak, despite its efforts to demassify, has yet effectively grappled with the true opportunities implied by its uniquely powerful network of distributors. It was George Hannye who pointed out to me that Kodak probably has the world's best distribution system, after Coca-Cola. You can go anywhere in the world, from East Timor to Timbuktu, and find Kodak film for sale. So what should Kodak do with this formidable capability?

As Eastman Kodak becomes liberated from pursuing declining businesses that historically have been corporate prisoners of the one-roof-over-everyone system, it can flexibly reposition some operations to capitalize on latent strengths. With the Kodak brand name and its tremendous distribution network, it is hard to imagine the company failing with new products that meet customer needs from region to region.

I believe that demass offers such flexibility, but each individual company, each CEO, must decide what's best for their company. There are too many possible approaches and potential traps to mention here. Nevertheless, I believe this outline is a good, serious start.

The operative word is serious. Bear in mind that what I've been discussing isn't a "program of the month," or another paperback "feel-good" philosophy. I cannot stress enough the need for an orderly change.

Do not allow initial problems to discourage you. There will be setbacks, but nothing should keep you from your goal of making your massive corporation flexible. Make its size work for you.

Demass is above all a business philosophy. It carries its own measure of risk for everyone, at all levels, including the CEO.

As businesspeople in their "own companies," employees within divisions and business units must come to know and understand the realities. Drum it into them. If it escapes, drum it in again. In this serious new world, productive product makers and support services providers get rewarded. Losers will be shut down, divested, or redefined.

The opportunity is an exciting one.

7
How Different Companies Have Demassified

Demassification comes in all shapes and sizes. Sometimes it's intentional; sometimes it isn't. Many companies are forced to overcome corporate gridlock in order to survive. Demassification to them is a process like guerrilla warfare, where victories are measured one liberated pocket at a time.

Demass sometimes is the result of keen vision and managerial diligence; other times it is the natural consequence of falling off a cliff.

The following is a sampling of companies that, in one dimension or another, embody one or more principles of demassification. None are demassified from top to bottom. In truth, no *Fortune* 500 company meets that description. The reason is that demassification, when it occurs, initially occurs inadvertently or on a laboratory experiment basis, as an example to the massified corporation of what can be. If given the right degree of executive support, these experiments have an exceptionally high success rate. But even with success, massified companies do not simply roll over and demassify.

One question puzzles me: Why do some large companies seem to do well, despite their mass? Milliken, the textiles giant, is one of the most centralized, most autocratically controlled organizations in the world. Yet the company is more flexible, and faster on its feet, than its competitors.

IBM suffers from massification more than most American corporations. Yet one of its plants won the 1991 Malcolm Baldrige National Quality Award. The same goes for General Motors, whose problems have been recounted in these pages, yet whose Cadillac Motor Car Division also won the Baldrige in 1991. How do I square this obvious success against the parent company's obvious "un-demassification"? The more I study the phenomenon, however, the more I am convinced that, lurking in the foreground of these massive corporations' structure, is something that gives these companies, or parts of them, the agility needed to survive.

At Milliken, that something appears to be an unsurpassable commitment to total quality management, which, because it empowers supervisors and line workers to make quality decisions, has the effect of counterbalancing the company's strong top-down orientation.

At IBM and General Motors, the Baldrige awards were made to divisions, not to the corporations themselves. I have visited IBM Rochester and was impressed at the amount of autonomy local units possessed. The plant boasted thousands of work teams, some consisting of only one or two members, many convened on an ad-hoc, let's-solve-this-problem-right-now basis. And Cadillac, which won the Baldrige not for making the world's best cars, but for making the biggest quality improvement, outstripped its parent company with an unremitting focus on understanding and meeting the needs of its customers.

That's not demass, but it's a spirit that drives responsibility for excellence to every employee's level so that everyone at every level and in every function is fixated on making and selling cars that people will want to buy and be happy to own. The net effect of this spirit is consonant with the effects of intentional demassification.

Demassification is a process much like guerrilla warfare, where victories are measured in pockets of liberation. Eastman Kodak is perhaps the most demassified *Fortune* 500 company, yet less than a third of its units have local responsibility, information, and accountability. Some of the companies cited in this chapter are still in the formative stages, but the successes in their "petri dishes" of demassification are very real. Each company has experienced in some part of its operations the futility of large-system thinking and applications, and has taken some steps to introduce small-scale information and management systems into its corporate structure.

Sometimes demassification turns on "downstaffing," trimming the corporate work force until a company is once again competitive on efficiency and price. Sometimes the pivotal action is junking the mainframe and installing a more intimate, computer-networked information system, with local ownership. Sometimes it is an extension of conventional decentralization — putting management muscle closer to the customer, where it can do the most good. In every case, constructive demassification must involve the genuine distribution of decision-making power and accountability for results to the people who must figure out the fine points of continuous improvement and are most motivated to put them into action.

EXAMPLES OF DEMASSIFIED COMPANIES

Asea Brown Boveri (ABB) is a $25 billion transportation-oriented company Americans know little about. The reason the public is unfamiliar with ABB is that it is a demassified international conglomerate: it is so thoroughly and radically decentralized that we simply lose sight of its mass.

ABB is the result of the mergers of two respected European firms: Asea of Sweden and Brown Boveri of Switzerland. Once merged, the new company went on an acquisitions spree. Today the company has a hand in 60 different companies and employs 240,000 people around the world.

There is nothing unique about being a multinational conglomerate. What sets ABB apart is that the company seems to have no center. Though nominally a Swiss company, it has a staff of only 100 managers in Zurich. With operations on every continent, it is truly a company with many homes, yet it does not see itself as a global company. Rather, it is an extended family of businesses, some of them very small and others more closely fitting the description of massiveness.

The company is built along business-unit lines. ABB sees itself as roughly 5,000 local "companies," each operating as a profit center, and each reporting to an executive committee. Business units are encouraged to manage themselves, according to the rules and realities of the countries each is doing business in, or with.

ABB is undaunted by the challenges of doing business across national boundaries. If doing business in a new country poses logistical problems, ABB simply forms a new business unit for that country.

For a large company, ABB can be sensationally entrepreneurial. When the Berlin Wall came down, ABB was there first, hiring people and making plans to put Eastern Europeans to work. It owns 3 companies in the former East Germany and is working on buying another 17. Because of its demassified structure, ABB feels it knows how to make these fledgling companies profitable while other companies are still learning the capitalist ropes.[1]

ABB does interesting things. It has made English its official corporate language. When CEO Percy Barnevik, a Swede, writes a letter to colleagues back in Sweden, the letter is in English. Every manager with a global role in the company must speak English. And yet, said Sune Karlsson, an ABB vice president, "we are not really a global business. We are a collection of local businesses with intense global coordination. This makes us unique. We want our local companies to think small, to worry about their home market and a handful of export markets, and to learn to make money on smaller volumes."

Teaming and empowerment are central to the conglomerate's success. And ABB does everything possible to guarantee job security for its workers.

Because the parent company buys in huge volumes — about $500 million annually — the myriad minicompanies have much more clout with suppliers than "actual" small competitors.

One of ABB's American companies, Rochester-based ABB Kent-Taylor, was one of the first ABB strategic business units (SBUs) to downsize, and therefore personalize, its information systems. "Demassification places significant expectations on each manufacturing unit," said Sondra Berry, director of information services at ABB Kent-Taylor.

"Suddenly, each SBU becomes solely responsible for its success or failure. Decision-making power moves from the tower to the trenches. And sound decisions require timely access to useful data. Timely and useful weren't even in the mainframe's vocabulary."

What ABB has done is create a workable model for every large corporation: remove the glut of management at the top; transform central management from autocrats to orchestrators; designate money-making operations as intimately and as locally as possible; and then give them the information, the tools, the training, and the muscle to succeed.

"Someone asked me if my ultimate goal is to create 5,000 little Percy Barneviks, one for each of our profit centers," Barnevik told *Harvard Business Review*.[2] Barnevik laughed and said no, out of modesty. But in fact, a demassified company comprises a number of mini-COOs — Barneviks, if you will — one per independent business unit. The payoff is liquidity, flexibility, and competitiveness throughout the world.

Perhaps no American corporation in the past decade has set itself as brisk a pace of change as Xerox Corporation, headquartered in Stamford, Connecticut. Xerox invented xerography, or photocopying, and never looked back, going on to become a large and prosperous company. But in the 1970s it visibly stumbled. Competitors, including Fuji and Kodak, suddenly poured through the flank of what had been a near-monopoly business. And Xerox was humbled as some of the technologies it had created at its world-class research and development center, Xerox PARC, went on to make billions — for other companies.

Despite its genius, Xerox found itself in trouble. The story of the company's resurgence under then-chairman David Kearns, its dynamic Leadership Through Quality program, and its eventual winning of the Malcolm Baldrige National Quality Award in 1990, is part of American business lore.

But the total quality management revolution at Xerox was only one dimension of its overhaul. In February 1992, CEO Paul A. Allaire announced a restructuring to force power down through the corporate ranks. "What we're telling people is that this is the biggest thing since Leadership Through Quality," Allaire said. The new corporation would contain only three management levels:

1. Corporate, headed by Allaire, would manage the company's finances, set policy, allocate resources, and chart overarching strategies.
2. Business was composed of nine autonomous, product-oriented business divisions and three autonomous, service-oriented customer operations divisions. Each business division was to decide which products to make, how to make them, what to charge, and how to service the equipment and bill customers.
3. Operational, the level closest to Xerox customers, would be responsible for day-to-day business and customer operations.[3]

Demassification isn't going to happen to Xerox overnight. A company spokesperson conceded that its population of general managers took decades to swell to its current size. But the new plan should eventually cut through the corporate fat and pay dividends in terms of flexibility and speed. Under the Xerox plan, said a company spokesman, "No job will have two bosses, much less three. We are going to develop an organization that is flexible, fast-moving, entrepreneurial and empowering of people. People talk a lot about these things. We're going to do it."

The story of Caterpillar, Incorporated, is one of the most painful success stories in recent memory. In the early 1980s the company was on the brink of annihilation in the world marketplace, locked in mortal combat with Komatsu to decide which would be king of the earth-mover business. By all rights, it should have been Caterpillar, which originated the idea of placing crawler tracks on heavy vehicles to make them move more easily through rugged terrain. In the early days, they thought they were in the farm implement business; they most decidedly were not. Without Caterpillar, there would have been no tanks in World War I. Using tractors for construction occurred to the company much later, partly because military tanks were enlisted as road-building tools in the 1920s.

Once the company was positioned as a maker of earthmoving equipment, its destiny was secure, for a while at least. It was a traditional, unpretentious, no-nonsense place to work, with an aptitude for quality unparalleled in American industry. The great irony, in fact, was that the Japanese made such great inroads against a company that had never succumbed to a decline in product quality. Even as the company staggered through the 1980s, no one took shots at Caterpillar's quality. But the company lost hundreds of millions of dollars through this period and underwent an agonizing reduction and restructuring of its work force as the construction industry dried up, and Komatsu's cheaper, smaller machines stole market share.

Caterpillar saw the writing on the wall. Quality alone was no longer enough; flexibility had become the name of the game. Though larger than Komatsu ($11 billion to $6 billion in sales), Caterpillar knew it had to compete on flexibility or go under. The challenge was to draw itself up another notch, to become a world-class manufacturer.

Caterpillar understood that the key to upgrading was employee involvement, and as a first step it decentralized into 13 profit centers based in the plants. The original idea was simple enough: to move design engineers from a single central location out into the divisions. But the process didn't stop there. Donald Fites, Caterpillar's new president and a global business manager (he speaks German, Japanese and Portuguese), found himself saying, "Hey, wait a minute, why just the manufacturing and engineering people?"

Before Fites was done, he'd picked up corporate headquarters and shaken the box until just about everyone came tumbling out, including marketers and pricing people. Soon everyone was working closely together on site, in a kind of family configuration. The payoff was immediate. In inventory alone, Caterpillar discovered that it had been stumbling blindly in the dark. In the old days, parts stacked up for weeks in one plant waiting to be heat treated. Then they were shipped long distance to another plant for milling, drilling, and final assembly. The people at the two sites were performing their jobs almost perfectly, but being 250 miles apart wasted weeks of time and increased the chances of parts getting banged up in transit.

With the new emphasis on incentives and ownership came a new employee/employer relationship. The company established a profit-sharing plan through the United Auto Workers and instituted a program called the Employee Satisfaction Process that involved job-floor workers in the everyday quality and decision-making processes. The old company virtues of integrity and optimism resurfaced as responsibility and partnership. A leaner, meaner, and greener Caterpillar soon found itself hiring again.

Even Ford Motor Company, which has been criticized over the years for its overcentralization, has made important strides in demassifying, at least within specific teams. In the 1980s, Ford decided to simulate a highly competitive, non-hierarchical, "practically Japanese" enterprise. The result was Taurus.

For years Ford had hewed to the tried-and-true centralized practices of American car making. "Team Taurus" replaced Ford's traditional top-down organizational structure. You know — design it here, pass it on to engineering, have the numbers people take it apart, and then shove it down the long table toward production. Every cog in the machine worked in isolation, with little communication, and no one person with overall project responsibility.

Team Taurus tried something new, mixing all their people and processes together from the start and forging strong communications and ownership links between groups. Ford designers pulled a card from the Japanese deck, and did some "reverse engineering" of their own. They took apart a Honda Accord and Toyota Corolla, piece by piece, each time looking for things they could improve on. They brought in assembly line personnel and asked their opinions on improving quality, productivity, and even design. And Ford brought its vendors into the process, decreasing the atmosphere of short-term competitiveness and signing on the best to long-term contracts.

The Ford plant in Chicago, which was originally built to assemble Model T's, was never thought of as "state of the art" in any way. It nevertheless had defied experts by streamlining itself for higher productivity, more efficient inventory management, and a reputation for quality that leads the multinational corporation. The revamping cost of $200 million, thanks to the plant's team approach and to a nifty bit of automotive design, turned out to be a bargain.[4]

The overall process, which Ford dubbed "program management," was Ford's version of demassified manufacturing. And it was a smashing success for Ford, and the first indication since the debacle of 1981 that a massive car company could compete with strongly decentralized competitors abroad. The Taurus/Sable plant in Atlanta was likewise refurbished and instilled with a new team attitude. Industry watchdog Harbor & Associates has called Ford-Atlanta "the most efficient Big Three auto plant." This, even though Ford-Atlanta is 42 years old!

Is Ford Motor a demassified corporation? Not by a long shot. Even at its successful Chicago plant, Ford failed the critical demassification test of putting information systems into the possession of the business units that actually use the information. But it was a remarkable leap forward. It was part and parcel of a serious corporate effort to move beyond lip service about quality and competitiveness, and to try their hand at the real thing. This seriousness was borne out by a 1991 study by *Automotive Industries* magazine, which found that Ford, as a whole, was the most efficient of the Big Three American car makers and that its production efficiencies put it close to the high standards set by their Japanese competitors. The study, which measured North American plant productivity according to workers per car per day, showed Ford trailed Asian transplants by only 2.7 percent. Chrysler and GM finished far behind.

Ford's experiments with Taurus and Sable in Chicago and elsewhere are a sign that even the biggest of giants can learn to dance a different step.

Teledyne, Incorporated, has been one of the more successful and unconventional conglomerates in American business today. It is a collection of business units that operate autonomously, are geographically scattered, and have many different product strategies. It is the number-one producer, for instance, of dental irrigators, swimming pool heaters, and zirconium!

Founded by Henry Singleton and George Kozmetsky in 1960, and headquartered in Los Angeles, the company is best known for the Water Pik. But Singleton, an unusually keen-eyed entrepreneur, involved Teledyne from its earliest days in a variety of other businesses: microcircuits, electronic guidance and navigation systems, remote-controlled airplanes, engines, machine tools, offshore oil platforms, tires, zirconium and hafnium (materials essential to operating nuclear reactors), tungsten, molybdenum, insurance, banks, and savings and loans.

By one measure the company is still massively centralized — as of 1992, Henry Singleton, though retired in 1989, is still the largest shareholder and company's guiding light. No one is complaining about this. Teledyne stock has been one of the bargains of the century — $1,000 invested in the company 30 years ago would have grown to over $50,000 today.

Still, several of its companies have had problems getting their product out the door in a timely fashion. Its thriving business unit, Teledyne Water Pik, was divided into two Colorado locations, employing over 700 people. But the two sites were getting their wires crossed on a regular basis. The plant that provided plastic-molded parts for assembly to the other plant was falling behind, and the existing computer system, an aging mainframe, was unable to bring the two plants together in anything like a dialogue. Management couldn't see that at the time; all it saw was that schedules were falling behind and costs were rising. The move to a downsized system was undertaken mainly to trim excess costs from its information services budget.

The side effects of downsizing their corporate computer system were pleasant surprises to Teledyne. The personal computer-based MRP II system they installed had the same depth of capability as their old mainframe — the bills of material capability was 99 levels deep! "We have always been a high-volume manufacturer," said Rick Weitzel, VP-MIS at Teledyne Water Pik. "We did not want to be tied down to a lot of shop paper. The microcomputer-based system we switched to helped us avert that fate."[5]

Installation was relatively easy; the entire systems implementation process was completed within seven months. Halfway through that period, several goals were achieved. Physical inventory variance was reduced to less than one-tenth of 1 percent. Long-term supplier contracts were expanded to unlimited planning capabilities, where the old mainframe system offered planning capabilities for only 16 weeks. Supplier purchase order production time was reduced from three to seven days to overnight. Materials variance was significantly improved.

"We now know where our inventory is and what stage of production it is in," Weitzel said. "Our mainframe system was completely incapable of this basic, essential communications task." He said that much of the inventory improvement stemmed from employees on the plant floor who now had a sense of ownership over their data. "Ultimately they know that they are responsible for our production numbers, our quality control, our success."

No discussion of demassified companies can long avoid the subject of International Business Machines Corporation's recent restructuring ordeal. IBM has been, of course, the great American company of the postwar era, eventually displacing General Motors as the quintessential symbol of big, modern, enlightened, blue-chip, "decentralized" but nevertheless massive business. The truth is, IBM has been drawn to decentralization like a moth to a flame. IBM seems to restructure every now and then just for the heck of it. During the 1980s, the company took great strides to become leaner and more flexible, shedding some 55,000 jobs through early retirements.

But those periodic changes didn't have much effect. By 1991, all the fun had gone out of standard decentralization. In November of that year, following a $3 billion write-off, an anxious Chairman John Akers released his now-famous memo. "The fact that we're losing market share makes me damn mad!" he said. He blasted lazy employees and threatened to undo the permissive, no-layoffs company culture.

Sure enough, by month's end, Akers ordered 20,000 employees stripped from the organization and implemented a major decentralization effort whose objective was to "create an environment where individual businesses will become as independent and autonomous as possible."[6]

Central management, under the Akers plan, will set financial goals for business units but will allow them to decide how to achieve them. "We will be taking a series of steps to enable each business unit to better focus on its own opportunities, be more responsive to its customers and accountable for its results," Akers said.

Akers described a "portfolio management" approach to a new IBM. The business unit concept would be taken seriously, and Akers held out the hope that each line of business could exist as a separate subsidiary. "We will review them to see how they are doing. Those that are attractive, we will invest in more aggressively. Those that are less attractive, we will invest in less aggressively," he said. "Managers who fail to meet profit targets will likely hit the street. Business units that come up short will most likely be sold off, chopped up, or closed down."

It all sounded great — a lot like demass, in fact. Except one important element was missing: downsizing information-processing technology, this time on the product end. IBM has been blessed over the years with many opportunities, and perhaps the greatest of them all was the bonanza of mainframe computer market dominance for the 40 years following World War II. Even today, with the company staggering from quarter to quarter, mainframes still provide most of the profits to the company's bottom line. But the mainframe market stopped growing years ago. Though IBM had an important part in lending credibility to microcomputers when it unveiled its first PC in 1981, PCs have never been the moneymaker that mainframes were.

For years, IBM has been upstaged in the strategically important PC market by companies that sell them for a third of IBM's price. IBM relinquished technological leadership and became a company driven, not by the market, but by marketing itself.

For IBM to succeed in demassifying will require a shift so dramatic, and so out of keeping with its own nature — it is both the emperor and the slave of large systems — that it is almost out of the question. IBM's dramatic reorganizational plan is simply not as dramatic as it needs to be. The company has agreed to decentralize into 50,000-employee entities; but not to radically decentralize into empowered, independent, 200-250 employee business units.

Moving reporting lines around is not enough. Putting large and massive business units at arm's length and telling the new leader, "It's up to you to figure out how to succeed," is not enough, either. It's not enough because, in the ranks, where those IBMers closest to the customers work daily, not much has changed. New IBM leaders, even highly capable leaders, have been empowered. But the opportunity for true employee empowerment has again been passed over.

A company that was making extraordinary progress toward demassification was NCR Corporation, under chairman and CEO Charles E. Exley. More than any other executive, Exley, while at NCR, understood and was committed to working toward a demassified structure and a "street-of-shops" configuration. NCR merged with American Telephone & Telegraph Company in 1991, and when that happened, I naturally concluded that demassification there had come to a halt. AT&T, after all, is one of the most monolithic and centralized corporations there has ever been. But perhaps there is room to hope. Robert E. Allen, CEO of AT&T, seems to be committed to transmitting power down through the lines. Two of his first acts were to slash 24,000 jobs from payroll and to decentralize the deregulated company into 20 separate business lines. To communicate his vision of the quicker, more responsive corporation, he turned the flowchart upside down, putting himself and other corporate officers in subordinate or supporting positions relative to business-unit presidents. The quest for flexibility has led Allen to further decentralization, handing over responsibility for day-to-day operations to a five-person Operations Committee, of which he is not a member.[7]

It is too soon to say how AT&T will go. Few expect that it will go the "street-of-shops" route. Yet if a supercentralized company like AT&T can rethink itself, and has committed, through its merger to NCR, to technology downsizing, anything is possible.

It is somewhat of a paradox, but the hallmark of manufacturing at Houston's Cooper Industries — a diversified conglomerate making a bewildering array of transformers, compressors, pumps, drapery hardware, hand tools, drills, computer cable, and oilfield equipment — has always been simplicity. CEO Robert Cizik, in his 30-year term at the helm, has assembled more than 60 manufacturing companies.

Like Teledyne, Cooper Industries follows the model of heavy decentralization: compact central management, with a strong degree of divisional autonomy. But Cizik takes his lead from no one; he has crafted his own tough standards for a company that "thinks small in order to grow big." His precepts sound like a roll call of the hoary business doctrines of bygone days. Some have the sound of demass:

- Stick to your knitting. Manufacturers should manufacture, and let the service sector fight over their piece of the pie. Cizik believes in remaining close to markets, and doing the bulk of his business here in the United States. He would rather save money through creative downstaffing and efficiencies here at home than go for the short-term cost savings of offshore operations.[8]
- When you plan global top-down actions, like acquisitions or five-point productivity improvement schemes,

do yourself a favor. Call in the people who know most about the business in question — your plant managers. Empowered managers are a CEO's most powerful tool.

- Diversify into business lines whose cycles offset one another. A good example of this was his acquisition of Champion Spark Plug — when the primary auto market goes down, he makes hay with aftermarket offerings. Many small, autonomous, free-standing business units that are scattered geographically give a company more flexibility than a handful of business lines under one grand roof.

Good rules, all. But Cizik has one overriding law preempting all the others: *stay lean*. Consider that Cooper Industries has been around more than 150 years, that it enjoys annual sales in excess of $6 billion, that it manufactures an astounding 2 million different products, with plants in 28 states and 19 countries. Now, guess the size of his corporate staff. The answer is 350. "I like my executives stretched," says Cizik with a smile.

The process, often called "Cooperizing," reflects the active paradox at work at Cooper Industries: strong central controls, but with equally strong accountability for business units up and down the corporate flowchart. Cooper Industries is well known for its insistence on small businesses with strong central controls. Over 22 "companies" have been designated by the parent company as business units. They include names like Ajax, Baron Drawn Steel, Champion Aviation, Anco, Belden, and Kirsch.

In 1991 I asked Cooper's management where the company stood with regard to world markets, and where it wanted to be. Their answers are like a bellwether for business organizations of the future.

Management sees its greatest strength in the years ahead as manufacturing flexibility. They believe strongly in benchmarking. Each Cooper business has a pretty good idea of what the competition is doing. Cooper's top managers feel they are making the kinds of quality improvements and cost reduction moves needed to stay competitive, even against companies abroad. The one benchmarking category in which Cooper management felt uncomfortable was in comparing themselves to competitors in total cycle time to market, a lingering problem for the company.

Though Cooper managers don't use the word, demass has been the single defining characteristic of Cizik's unique, no-frills management style. His companies know what is expected of them, and he provides them with the systems and training to perform. With the "think small" approach, Cooper Industries is taking aim at a level of achievement most large manufacturing companies don't dare dream of: reducing waste, speeding production, and increasing earnings to match the flexibility and profitability of companies a fraction its size.

Thomas J. Lipton, Incorporated, means tea to most people. In fact, Lipton introduced packaged tea to the tea-drinking capital of the world, Great Britain. The face on the package of Lipton Tea is actually Sir Thomas Lipton, a sailing enthusiast knighted by Queen Victoria who, on his many journeys abroad, snapped up every tea plantation in Ceylon, nearly cornering the world market.

Today, Lipton is the world's number-one seller of tea and dry soups. In addition, it owns food brands as well known and as diverse as Cup-A-Soup, Wish-Bone, Equal, Good Humor, Knox, Sunkist, Lawry's, and Wyler's. The company is actually a subsidiary of Unilever, Britain's largest consumer products company. But Lipton operates in most respects independently of its owner.[9]

Now, you might not think that Lipton, offering 1,400 different products, would have the manufacturing problems of the complexity of, say, Ford Motor. A pinch of this, a little of that, and it's suddenly spaghetti, right? But over the years, Lipton labored with a number of different large centralized manufacturing systems, some of them good at basic accounting, but none of them capable of keeping intelligent track of inventory.

According to Martin Visagie, manager of exports and logistics development at Lipton's Toronto offices, their previous minicomputer was lacking in functionality, expensive to apply, and too costly to maintain. In 1987, under Visagie's direction, Lipton downsized to a personal computer-based manufacturing system, starting with the recently acquired Ragú spaghetti sauce plant in Peterborough, Ontario.

After about a week of false starts, the downsized system finally kicked in, and the benefits were soon apparent. Data was suddenly reliable because it was accurate — garnered and entered at the shop-floor level rather than passed down sacramentally from the remote mainframe. The personal computer system eventually succeeded in reducing raw materials inventories 35 percent and finished goods inventories 8 percent — all while sales were increasing at an annual clip of 10 percent. The company had been on the verge of installing yet another expensive, but seemingly indispensable mainframe software solution. But this downsized, locally operated system surprised everyone by solving the company's most pressing information problems, on a hamburger budget. Managers at the Ragú plant bubbled with delight. Their manufacturing information was better than they ever believed it could be. Within months, Lipton corporate management announced intentions to follow suit, and downsize an additional four sites.

As makers of superminicomputers and other high-powered, small-package computer products, Harris Corporation comes to demassification from several points at once — both as a company catering to demassification efforts of other companies, and as one waist-deep in the process itself.

Harris has had a challenging time of it in the 1980s and 1990s. It possessed technology and market niches that larger companies, like IBM and Unisys, would have loved to get their hands on. Indeed, Harris played the takeover and acquisitions game itself, at one point contemplating the acquisition of Digital Equipment and actually purchasing Lanier Products in 1983, an important addition to Harris's profit capabilities.

Harris had most of the problems of small, overmatched companies, along with most of the management and manufacturing hassles of its larger counterparts. The Lanier acquisition, which combined the flamboyant, fast-talking style of Lanier with Harris's traditional low-key approach, helped solve the problem of being too small. But it created the opposite problem — that of being too big.

Harris's solution — radical decentralization — gave the company new leverage, both on the factory floor and in the marketplace. As Herbert McCauley, VP of information management at Harris, put it, the company's philosophy is that "Small Is Better."

McCauley is no neophyte in the technology wars. He does double duty these days, working for Harris and serving as chairman of the Information Systems and Technology Council for the American Management Association. His background includes 15 years heading Harris's information program plus stints at such data-wise companies as Polaroid, Digital Equipment, and IBM. McCauley describes demass at Harris Corp. as employee empowerment and a "stretch preference for distributive computing."

The stretch preference means that Harris knows that whatever information-management products exist on the market today, existing features never fully satisfy evolving requirements. In the case of personal computers, local-area networks, and file server technology, most were marginally adequate in the mid-1980s. Yet that was when Harris committed to a distributive information system based on the educated premise that microcomputer architectures were the wave of the future and would soon come into their own. With the advent of Intel's 386 and 486 computer chips and multiprocessor-based servers, and the adoption of Novell's and other networking standards, the architecture did indeed fulfill its promise. Today, Harris boasts one of the most user-friendly, affordable, and efficient manufacturing systems in the industry.

A number of years ago, a Harris manufacturing center in Nashua, New Hampshire (since spun off) was faced with the challenge of gearing up for production of two major product lines. The writing was on the wall: change the way you do business or fail. Here was a division employing about 350 people, fabricating about 750 deliverable products from about 10,000 procured parts, doing production planning and control over telephone lines hooked up to two corporate mainframes, in order to run a mainframe-oriented manufacturing software setup. And how, with that complex setup, did they decide to improve manufacturing? By reaching down to more intimate technologies. They installed a personal computer-based manufacturing planning and control system.

The result? "Information-processing downsizing was a natural fit for us," McCauley said, "given our dedication to focused factories, cellular operations, just-in-time, total quality management, and distributive systems. Moving to a micro system as early as we did was a calculated risk that the technology and performance would be there when we needed it." What began as a run-of-the-mill decentralization into divisions, he said, curiously metamorphosed into something much more powerful — decentralization *within* divisions, organized around customer needs and changing market trends.[10]

"In the old days, we used to think of a great restaurant as a place with a menu that went on forever," McCauley said. "But we've moved beyond that. A great manufacturer is like this new view of a quality restaurant. Each day is a new and limited menu. But the focus and concentration on those few entrees is very great. And the experience is marvelous."

Swedish-owned Electrolux is the undisputed world champion in the home appliance business. It's a going concern, with annual sales in the $10-12 billion range, and operations in 50 countries. The company was founded by a Swedish business hero, Axel Wenner-Gren, who is one of the all-time great promoters. He once talked the Pope into using Electrolux for a year, free of charge, to keep the Vatican Palace free of dust — a publicity bonanza.

This original door-to-door vacuum cleaner company owns more brand names today than most people realize: White, Philco, Westinghouse, Regina, Gibson, Eureka, Kelvinator, Merritt, Frigidaire, Tappan. One name they do not own, at least in the U.S., is Electrolux itself; they lost control over their own flagship brand in 1968 when they sold off their interest in Consolidated Foods (now Sara Lee, though even that company has since spun off the Electrolux vacuum brand in a management buyout).

Electrolux is a no-nonsense business with an aggressive attitude toward its conglomerate components. If they do not occupy a number-one or number-two position in their respective markets, the axe is poised to fall.

Electrolux is out for results, not a protracted marriage with futureless businesses. Fix them, close them, or sell them; those are the three fates awaiting companies that, given the tools and autonomy to succeed, fail.

The company is divisionalized into six mega-areas — household appliances, commercial appliances, commercial services, outdoor products, industrial products, and building components. But each division is in turn broken up into dozens and dozens of smaller units, companies in their own right, with accountability for profits and costs. The arrangement gives this large, 200,000-employee company, with operations in 50 countries, surprising agility within its many market niches.

Information services has been completely demassified. "It was too cumbersome and expensive to try to tie all our small- to medium-sized manufacturing units into a central data processing system," said Kurt Gladh, VP of information services. "Our belief has always been that we will prosper as long as we think of Electrolux as a family of companies rather than one large one."

In general, the response of the newly accountable, newly responsible units has been impressive. Each unit now has its own personal computers connected into a local-area network-based information system. Each unit creates and manages its own data. Each unit within each business tracks its own financial progress toward meeting plan. It is a clear-eyed, white-knuckled, globally minded, sink-or-swim, entrepreneurially driven company.

The succession of changes at Electrolux prompted quality guru Joseph Juran (never generous with praise) to acknowledge the company publicly. "Electrolux decided it wanted to cut service calls in half in two years. They achieved this by breaking the service process down into the smallest possible components, examining them, and making incremental improvements. Bit by bit, by thinking small, they made major improvements. That's putting quality into the business plan. We find this thinking in every company that makes great strides."[11]

Instances of demassification in U.S. and global industries go on, but the trail takes many circuitous twists and turns. It is easy to think of companies that meet one or more of the five conditions of demassification: (1) They must be decentralized to the lowest possible level (2) with the greatest possible degree of flexibility, (3) the highest possible level of local autonomy, (4) competent personnel, and (5) the right tools to do the job.

Decentralization, the first condition, is an established concept, though few companies have taken it to the degree outlined in these pages. Any company worth its salt will claim it is working hard to achieve conditions 2, 4, and 5. Well-run conglomerates and holding companies have always understood the value of condition 3. I can't take credit for constructing these fundamental concepts of flexibility, empowerment, training, or appropriate technology. Well-managed companies have been pushing toward these goals for years.

Motorola has blazed a new pathway showing how big companies can learn to behave more like smaller companies, reducing total cycle time, nearly eliminating defects, and increasing operating efficiencies. Great "people" companies like Milliken and Federal Express have taught us about the importance of team building, quality training, and computer applications. Lockheed, Westinghouse, and Rockwell International have set new standards for accountability to the customer. General Electric and Baxter have put new spring in the step of large, multifaceted companies. Even quality improvements at the Buick and Cadillac divisions at General Motors are fresh signs that acting small and thinking big pays off. Great companies, all of them — nearly all, anyway. And remarkably successful, considering the disadvantage their size gives them. None have been completely demassified, though many programs, like GE chairman Jack Welch's efforts to "de-boundarize" his company, are heading in that direction.

True demass cannot be disguised, not even in a corporate flowchart a mile long. It is apparent in the companies' results: new relationships between central management and independent business units, lower costs, enhanced morale, and improved earnings for shareholders.

8
Demassification, Quality, and Flexibility

Quality is something we all know, in our hearts, should be simple. Just do it right. Or, if you make a mistake, fix it before you pass it on. Large American companies, shocked at Japanese quality performance, rushed to jump-start top-down-driven quality programs. Not one worked as hoped. Could mass and the communication problems that go with it be the major cause of inferior quality?

The impact of demassification on quality. As often happens in the quality movement, one discovery tends to anticipate and usher in another. In my mind there is not a great deal of daylight between the principle of quality in industry and the principle of radical decentralization. Like the chicken and the egg, the relationships between quality and ownership of information are inextricably intertwined.

In the age of massive centralization, quality has been little more than an ideal, something to be given only lip service, a vague entity sandwiched somewhere between engineering and marketing. Early forays into quality are something of an embarrassment to quality professionals today. Quality was seen as something added to a product, or stamped on after manufacture. At its worst, it was marketing hype, not a manufacturing strategy; extrinsic, not intrinsic; an afterthought.

Quality showed up primarily in jingles and logos on billboards, but infrequently in the products themselves. It took time and competition from abroad for American companies to realize that improvement meant real change, in the attitude of management and workers, in the way information is distributed throughout an organization, and in the actual power structure of the corporation.

That is what demass is about — the infusion of accountability at the lowest possible corporate level, a change that is both structural and attitudinal. Demassification creates a manufacturing mind-set in which quality is no longer secondary. It is, in fact, the product or service your company is in business to deliver.

CENTRALIZATION AND QUALITY

Funny thing about quality: management of large companies get excited about the concept and they get on the phone to the nearest quality guru — a Deming or a Crosby or a Juran. The guru visits, takes a dim view of the way things are going, and chews everyone out. Properly chastened, the company puts into effect a 10-point total quality plan that is supposed to turn the whole company inside out, hangs banners from every yardarm, holds a few pep rallies, prints up a special company newsletter, sits back, and waits for great things to happen. And waits. And waits. And waits.

Perhaps the first month will see good results. Everyone's excited. Managers want their numbers to look good. The fresh blast of rhetoric manages to focus everyone's attention, temporarily. If the company has a Baldrige team appointed, that team is still rosy-cheeked and energetic.

But the quality movement is soon dead, and no one is quite sure why. Mr. Deming was so charismatic. We monitored all our processes. We had great attendance at our quality lectures. What the heck happened?

What probably happened was that the company set up too high a hurdle for its fledgling quality program to vault over — overcentralized management and overcentralized controls. The company was trying to shout quality into existence, from the top floor of the corporate skyscraper, all the way down through the subbasement. And even with the finest intentions way up in the penthouse, it just didn't work.

A brief history of quality. Companies learned a lot about quality in the past 30 years, much of it the difficult, education-by-error that tells you what doesn't work. Most companies today agree that the following things don't work:[1]

6 Things that Don't Work

Protectionism. Keeping imports out of your country does nothing to drive your business to greater achievements. Trade barriers are an admission of one's inability — and unwillingness — to compete.

Exhortation. Forget the speeches, slogans, banners, and bumper stickers. Quality responds to commitment, not blarney.

Awareness training. Better than exhortation but not by much. This approach amounts to quality lip service, which is OK, but by itself does not lead to meaningful action.

Training in tools. Statistical tools are wonderful, but a preoccupation with technology can distract a company from addressing problems.

Quality control circles. Work teams by themselves, without leadership from above, cannot solve large quality problems. Worse, management can make scapegoats of them.

More testing, more inspection. This throws money at quality problems and hides waste. True quality management is preventive, not reactive.

Finding out what works is an ongoing process. Although we're getting closer all the time, it's still an uphill struggle. To fully understand quality, we need to talk about the nature of it: what it is in the abstract, and how it works in reality.

It is doubtful that any concept has simultaneously engaged and confused American business more than quality. Definitions of quality multiply faster than rabbits, and there is considerable overlap. Combining the views of various quality experts, I have come up with a baker's dozen dimensions of quality:

13 Definitions of Quality

1. **Conformance to Specifications:** the traditional manufacturing-based approach — is the product what it was designed to be?
2. **Performance:** does the product do what it's supposed to do? Performance must be repeatable or its appeal to customers fades.
3. **Quick Response:** how long must a customer wait for you to make things right?
4. **Quick-Change Expertise:** a manufacturer's yardstick — how quickly can you tear down and set up equipment to make a product?
5. **Features:** does the product out-deliver competition in number of desirable features?
6. **Reliability:** will your product do what it promises day in and day out, for a reasonable product lifetime?
7. **Durability:** will your product outlast its competitors?
8. **Serviceability:** if it breaks is that it?
9. **Aesthetics:** arbitrary, yes, but part of the mix — the intangible and emotional nuances of product quality.
10. **Perceived Quality:** does it look like and feel like a "quality" product?
11. **Humanity:** does your product in any way harm, offend, or denigrate people at any stage of the chain of customers, from vendors to end users?
12. **Value:** do you provide excellence at an attractive price and an acceptable cost?
13. **Customer Satisfaction:** because it is a quality concept that is with us whether we admit it or not, and always will be.

David Garvin, in *Managing for Quality: The Strategic and Competitive Edge*, says that quality is something that we all know should be simple, but in real life is almost infinitely difficult. Philip Crosby used the slogan "Quality Is Free" and became world-famous, and his point is well taken: attention to quality costs little or nothing compared to the cost of bad quality. But a slogan is just a slogan. Beneath its surface tranquillity, the concept of quality roils and shimmers in a way that we at times seem almost incapable of perfectly understanding.

True quality — "Big Q" quality, in which quality is seen as an all-encompassing feature of business life (as opposed to "small-q" quality, which merely seeks conformance to specifications) — is the virtual religion of world-class manufacturing today. Like most religions it has its saints — W. Edwards Deming, Joseph Juran, Philip Crosby, and Armand Feigenbaum. It also has false prophets, people who hustle quality but are not themselves committed to it, or don't comprehend its implications.

In this century a true quality movement began primarily as a way to cut costs. Too many poorly made parts were showing up at the end of the assembly line. Too many assemblies and components were breaking down during testing. Too many finished products were coming back under warranty. Too many sales were lost because of the growing suspicion in the customer's mind that their supplier simply wasn't capable of turning out decent products.

Quality control was inserted, as an external element, into the midst of internal operations with the assignment of reducing those bad numbers. In the old days engineers with calipers stood at the end of the assembly line, sorting product into GO and NO GO piles. Production people were suspicious of them; management and finance people tended to dismiss them as mid-level kids sent to do an adult's job.[2]

By the early 1970s, inspection gave way to the quality assurance movement. Quality was now seen as a preventive concept rather than a curative concept. It was a *how* and no longer a *what.* Consultants were called in to help companies design industrial processes that would minimize errors. This was a big step forward in improved efficiencies since fewer mistakes meant lower costs and fewer unhappy customers. We thought we were working at a very advanced level in those days.[3]

And the idea survives very successfully today at companies that devote themselves to a singularly high level of product quality. Motorola, winner of the 1989 Malcolm Baldrige National Quality Award, describes its mission simply as the delivery of a product virtually free of defects, the elusive 6Σ — Six Sigma, standing for 99.9997 percent defect-free.

DEMASSIFICATION AND QUALITY

But the 1970s were the Stone Age compared to what was to come. The sudden rise of foreign competition was like a thunderclap for manufacturers. It got their attention, in a hurry, putting manufacturers on notice that quality-as-cost-containment structure was penny-ante stuff. Sure, by internal measures, American companies had improved over their own quality benchmarks since the fat and sassy '50s and '60s. But compared to the total quality and continuous improvement (*kaizen*) culture of the Japanese, we were light years behind, and the competition was killing us.[4]

Just-in-time. A powerful new concept — the most important innovation in manufacturing since mass production — arrived on these shores in the 1980s. It was called just-in-time. Shortened to JIT, it's a "flow" concept inspired by Deming's work in Japan and by the ideas of Taiichi Ohno, an engineer with Toyota. Thoughtful U.S. manufacturers seized quite correctly on the just-in-time operating philosophy, as a profit-minded pathway through the quality wilderness. The primary axioms of JIT are

- The smaller the lot size, the better.
- Buy and produce in small quantities.
- Commit to continuous improvement in manufacturing, with a minimum cushion of materials to keep production running.

JIT assails the concept of waste on every front, defining waste as *anything that does not add value*. Just-in-time, for example, was at the heart of Jack Philbin's efforts at Eastman Kodak to empty the huge automated warehouses that were dragging manufacturing down.

What exactly does it mean, to "add value"? That is the question that everyone involved in JIT manufacturing must continually ask. Consider the following activities, all of which conventional manufacturing is committed to. Which are essential to the business of making things, and how many are just tedious habits?

- counting it
- moving it
- storing it
- expediting it
- searching for it
- taking it out of one container, and putting it in another
- accumulating it into larger make/move quantities
- inspecting it

How mass impacts just-in-time. What we quickly see is that the activities we take for granted, because they have always been part of our manufacturing "system," are not intrinsic to manufacturing. Why do we overlook the overwhelming logic of striking these purposeless endeavors? Perhaps it is because the individuals who are most aware of the waste are not allowed to do anything about it — the consequences of manufacturing centralization and the "don't-do-anything-'til-headquarters-tells-you-it's-all-right" attitude.

JIT turns that attitude around and puts everyone in charge of improving processes. It is almost by definition a demassified concept of bottom-up quality improvement. Nevertheless, I sometimes think that in seizing on JIT, we overlook this commonsense dimension and focus too narrowly on JIT as a mechanical inventory-reduction scheme. It took years for it to dawn on us that inventory optimization — having the right stuff on hand at the right time, and not the rest of the time — is merely the front end of JIT.

The multiple dimensions of quality. Now an alphabet soup of quality-related terms swirls around us:

- JIT (just-in-time), improving total cycle time and inventory efficiency.
- EI (employee involvement), the idea that quality isn't the job of the person with the calipers, it's everyone's job.
- SPC (statistical process control), the continuous monitoring of all factory problems on charts.

What JIT, EI, and SPC led to was something almost invisible to the casual onlooker, yet remarkably grand in its implications: the idea that factory flexibility served the customer first, and the factory second. This concept would fire such groundbreaking studies as Richard Schonberger's *Building a Chain of Customers*. Schonberger's thesis is that there is more mileage left in the old phrase "customer driven" than most would guess. He redefines "customer" to mean virtually every participant in a company's workings that hands work off to another party — every department, division, and individual working to make that company succeed — as well as the traditional external customer who actually writes the check.[5]

Using Schonberger's chain of customers approach, it is possible to fashion our own map, or chain, of processes, that encourages improvement and efficiencies at every link. Where each hand reaches for the next, adding or subtracting value, that is where quality rises or falls in manufacturing, not by the edicts or whims of centralized management.

Total quality management (TQM). The evolution from quality control to today's TQM was clearly linked by the quality theories of Armand Feigenbaum. In the 1950s, Feigenbaum, a disciple of statistical process control pioneer Walter Shewhart, proposed that quality may begin in the manufacturing area, but logically had to extend to every dimension of the way a company does business — it must be total.

TQM includes quality of goods, services, time, place (buildings, plants, offices), equipment and tools, processes, people, environment and safety, information, and measurements. TQM means an unending series of checks on every aspect of business, at each link of the business chain, on people, tools, and processes. When things don't check out, TQM means stopping, searching out the cause, and fixing it. Only when the system has been corrected should processing restart.

TQM means approaching quality in two statistically different ways: one is the average level of quality of a product or process; the other, the variability around that average. With these two numbers in hand, manufacturers finally have the kind of benchmarks they need to turn vague notions of quality into a powerfully specific instrument of control.

The reason TQM works is that it finds a way to link employees with a dimension they are seldom exposed to — an organization's strategy. As Richard Pascale says in *Managing on the Edge*:

> It is hard to enlist passionate commitment among employees to a "strategy." The goal of "penetrating markets via price or feature differential" may quicken the pulse of MBAs, but it leaves most employees cold. "Strategy" is too cerebral. In contrast, "quality," like "crisis," appeals to people because they can relate to it. Everyone, at every level can do something about it and feel the satisfaction of having made a difference. Making products that work or providing first-class service is something we can identify with from our own experience.
>
> Equally significant, "quality" can be quantified. This has intrinsic appeal to engineering, operations, finance, and other numbers-oriented groups who only tend to take things seriously when they can be pinned down.[6]

The beauty of Baldrige. When Congress established the Malcolm Baldrige National Quality Award in 1987, total quality management became part of the official fabric of quality in the United States. The award plainly calls for a participative approach to management, requiring quality leadership at the top, but quality action welling up from the lower ranks as well.

The Baldrige Award is essentially an essay test, asking 36 questions about a company (or company division) in seven key areas:

Leadership
Information and Analysis
Strategic Quality Planning
Human Resource Development and Management
Management of Process Quality
Quality and Operational Results
Customer Focus and Satisfaction

There was initially a great deal of skepticism about the award. Would it be heavy on the window dressing and light on the nuts and bolts of true quality assurance? If it was a test, what questions would be asked? Who would ask them? Who would decide whether the answers were right? Worse, would the largest corporate contributors to the Foundation for the Malcolm Baldrige National Quality Award waltz away with the statuettes every year? Fortunately, management of the Baldrige process was assigned to the National Institute of Standards and Technology (formerly the National Bureau of Standards), long recognized as strictly impartial.

Just as important to getting the Malcolm Baldrige Award off to a good start was the selection of Curt Reimann to head it. Reimann found himself in the unusual position of having to define quality to American business in a way that companies could not only agree with, but would also feel motivated to attain. To help resolve this dilemma, Reimann fashioned a list of "Seven Essentials" — seven dynamics that must be in place for a company to even be in the Baldrige ballpark.

7 Essentials

- Continuous improvement in all areas and operations
- Accurate measurement of improvements
- A business plan that benchmarks your company's performance against world-class companies
- A true partnership with both vendors and customers, creating a continuous feedback loop to drive continuous improvement
- A profound commitment to knowing and meeting customer needs
- A commitment not just to fixing mistakes but to preventing them
- Quality-based leadership that touches an organization at every level, from top to bottom

Source: Curt Reimann

Juran took Reimann's seven essentials a few steps further. In 1991 his researchers at Juran Institute analyzed the experiences of every Baldrige winner to date, looking for "common indicators of quality." This analysis showed that most Baldrige winners had implemented nearly every one of these 15 actions.

Baldrige is profoundly transforming the way we manufacture in this country. Baldrige creates a common language and a common standard for quality. It takes the hodgepodge of slogans, concepts, and dogmas that have peppered the quality landscape and unifies them under a single rubric. As a consequence, many different things have started to happen on the quality scene, all of them good. The not-so-hidden agenda of the Baldrige Award was to alter the dimensions of quality education in America. Baldrige gave companies and consultants a common curriculum and a shared understand-

15 Things that Do Work

- Make "customer focus" a major element of your quality strategy.
- Follow the "Big Q" principle, addressing the needs of internal as well as external customers.
- Adopt the concept of mandated, annual quality improvement at a revolutionary pace. This means making hundreds, even thousands of quality improvements every year.
- Create an infrastructure to identify what must be improved, and assign clear responsibility for making these improvements.
- Assign clear ownership for managing the multifunctional business processes, and define necessary responsibilities.
- Undertake projects to improve the business processes. Shorten the time to provide customer service, reduce cycle times for launching new products, lower error rates, and so on.
- Involve those who will be affected by the plan in the planning. Adopt modern, quality-oriented methodology to replace empiricism.
- Include suppliers in the planning as well. Convert adversarial relationships to ones based on teamwork. Reduce the number of suppliers and increase the life span of contracts.
- Train all members of the management hierarchy to be proficient in the three quality management processes: planning, control, and improvement.
- Revise processes at the worker level so the workers can supervise themselves.
- Allow the work force to participate actively on quality improvement teams.
- Establish test sites to train worker teams and let the teams supervise themselves.
- Make changing behavior, not just providing education, the goal of training.
- Enlarge the business plan to include establishing quality goals, defining the actions needed to meet them, and setting clear responsibility for these actions.
- Establish "stretch" goals via benchmarking; base these goals on the results achieved in the same function by other leading companies.

Source: Joseph Juran

ing of what constituted total quality management, which stands at the very core of the Baldrige approach.

Companies like Ford have created their own version of the Baldrige, which they ask their vendors to submit to. And individual states, like Minnesota, have created mini-Baldriges. Europe, too, is imitating Baldrige with the European Quality Award, due to kick off in 1994, based on the ISO 9000 set of international quality standards.[7]

ISO 9000 is a foundational set of quality standards on which companies in any industry can create a quality system. Though instituted to create international standards for a united Europe, it has worldwide ramifications. Asia and North American companies are certifying their products for ISO 9000 in order to sell them in Europe. In so doing, they are finding that the standards are flexible and simple enough to use domestically as well.[8]

Baldrige fosters the development of a new level of communications within companies. Whereas in the past, companies may have encouraged departmental and divisional goal sharing, Baldrige escalates that dynamic by insisting on "cross-functional communications" — communications that break through old barriers and accepted boundaries, connecting team to team and level to level. Remarkably, we even see the creation of multi-industry Baldrige-based user groups. Baldrige helps create a culture of quality, like a well that companies can come to and draw from. The award establishes common values and common standards. It identifies and celebrates national models for other companies to learn from, imitate, follow, or just be inspired by. It creates a basis for flexible self-assessment that any company, or any part of any company, can use for its own internal purposes.

But Baldrige isn't perfect. Companies have complained that the criteria can be confusing; that the award is exploited by over-eager consultants; and that it is held hostage by its winners' future performance. What would happen to the award's prestige if award-winning Cadillac Motor Company has to recall 100,000 cars next month?

Tom Peters has criticized Baldrige because it doesn't acknowledge that *mass* in and of itself is a liability. "I got antsy when Motorola, IBM, and GM copped the lion's share of the manufacturing awards," Peters said. "I re-read the application — Baldrige is eerily silent about the need to get rid of bureaucracy in organizations. Despite remarkable gains, these three giants remain bureaucratic quagmires."[9]

Baldrige offers no reward for companies that make themselves leaner. In fact, it can be argued that the rigors of Baldrige-style self-assessment actually encourage the spread of centralized middle-manager sprawl.

Despite these quibbles, however, there is no denying that the Baldrige assessment is one of the most important business ideas of our time. Thousands of companies are learning that, regardless of the award itself, the criteria used in the award process provide a cohesive, unifying, and complete measuring stick for total quality management.

The "Nifty Fifty" and the "Magnificent Eight". Baldrige applies to all kinds of businesses, but there are also quality and performance standards just for manufacturing businesses. For this statistical dimension, many factory managers look to MRP II Class A Certification, which does a much better job addressing key issues of scheduling, conformance to specifications, and cycle time.

MRP II can be used to implement principles embedded in the Baldrige criteria. It can also be used with JIT, though some authorities disagree on this. Their feeling is that MRP II is incompatible with JIT. They define JIT as a "pull" system, meaning that parts and materials are moved only when someone needs it. This definition incorrectly equates JIT with *kanban*, the work line system Ohno pioneered at Toyota. And they define MRP II as a "push" system, meaning that it actually launches orders for parts and materials. Since push is the opposite of pull, JIT must be the opposite of MRP II.

The problem is that JIT is not at all identical to kanban; it is a much broader concept, encompassing the waste-elimination ideas of many people in addition to Ohno. JIT is more than a mechanical model; it is a philosophy of efficiency that should underlie manufacturing operations. MRP II, by contrast, is something more concrete, a planning technique that can admirably support a JIT or any other approach to manufacturing.

MRP II is, as has been noted, the "flow system" manufacturers use to plan and keep their manufacturing operations running. Based on a master production schedule, bills of material, and inventory position, MRP II calculates when shortages will occur and makes recommendations to avoid stockouts while maintaining minimum inventory. In most large companies, MRP II is run as computer software, but it is really an implementation of standards to keep manufacturers efficient and on track.

One of the chief benefits of an MRP II system is its ability to advise people to make the right items in the right quantities and to ship finished items on time. Customer service improves, and as a side benefit, inventories are reduced. After all, one of the best ways to reduce inventory is to get finished product out the door on schedule.

MRPII Class A Certification is a measurement methodology by which companies can call in outside expert observers to verify that the company is manufacturing at the highest level. Despite all the other prizes and awards out there, Class A Certification is vital for achieving world-class manufacturing excellence.

The beauty of the MRP II Class A Certification process lies in two features: the design of its metrics and the course of their implementation. Its design is open and, while the original criteria were developed by the Oliver Wight organization, there is no "set" group of 50 (or 100, or 150) criteria companies must follow.

Each company must streamline the ideas put forth by Wight to establish its own custom set of criteria that best reflect the realities and requirements of that business. This streamlining is done with the assistance of outside consultants to ensure that the eventual definition of excellence is more like hardball than slow-pitch softball.

The other feature is the implementation itself. Of the customary 50 or so performance criteria it examines and evaluates, Class A requires an overall total score of 90 percent plus a score in excess of 90 percent on the 8 most critical criteria. Examination is spearheaded by independent outside parties. Companies wishing to undertake this "trial by excellence" must first review the criteria to make sure they are applicable. From the lengthy list of 50 or so measures, special weight is usually given a handful of selected, overriding measures. Within Eastman Kodak these selected measures are called "The Magnificent Eight."

Here are Eastman Kodak's "Magnificent Eight":

The Magnificent 8

1. Delivery performance to customers must be equal to or greater than 95 percent.
2. Inventory accuracy must be equal to or greater than 95 percent.
3. Routing accuracy must be equal to or greater than 98 percent.
4. Accuracy of active bills of material must be equal to or greater than 98 percent.
5. Rough-cut capacity planning must be utilized.
6. Requirements must be communicated with suppliers beyond their lead time.
7. All people have gone through appropriate education.
8. Master production schedules are visibly managed/doable.

Source: Eastman Kodak Co.

Obsession or pride? Tom Peters asserted in *Thriving on Chaos* that quality must begin with emotion—management's emotion. And the emotional state that drives quality higher, he said, must be *obsession.*[10] I would like to build on that statement.

A campaign to build a fire of managerial obsessiveness misses the objective by half. It creates an image of mad-dog managers worrying the bone of quality long after the practical marrow has been sucked clean. Obsession is easy to fake and hard to sustain.

To me, the default emotion should be pride. This is the kind of pride that lies at the heart of demass: awareness of what your job is and what your coworker's job is, awareness that you have responsibility and accountability for what you produce.

Since what you do is constantly being measured, a little greed is thrown in here, along with a little fear. But more important than either of those is a calm alertness to tasks and objectives, and the knowledge that what you do makes a great deal of difference, and that shows up in the numbers. *Your* work, and *your* numbers.

9

The Human Factor

In order for demassification to work, three things must be in place. You must have employees with the basic smarts — whether by schooling or training — to understand their jobs. They must be empowered by top management. And they must be given the information and tools to do the job.

Demassification is a bold process because it threatens to upset the centralist applecart that all large companies push. Companies won't learn a new way to push unless something in turn is pushing them. Great change cannot occur during a time of corporate tranquillity. Demass is an option companies will entertain only when market circumstances threaten to bash the old applecart to smithereens.

To many employees, demass sounds like the latest in a series of corporate nightmares. They see it as headcount downstaffing for cost savings, period. They see it as a code word for upper management to use while sharpening its knives on the necks of middle managers.

But demass is a different kind of downsizing; it's a "rightsizing" of human resources, a rescaling of the way we think about utilizing a company's most valuable resources. Rightsizing human resources means empowerment. Everyone talks about empowerment, but talking is all they're doing. Making it actually happen is something else again. Taking decision-making authority that once resided on top of the corporate pyramid, and bringing it down to the individual worker is something few managers are eager to try. Those who do usually take back the power at the first sign of difficulty.

Ask Jack Philbin, who helped demassify Eastman Kodak, what demassification is, and he will say it is synonymous with empowerment. "Demassifying means putting power in the hands of the people who can most effectively use it."

THE MASSIFIED MANAGER

Some managers naturally resist any kind of empowerment. They fear it will undermine their position. If people working under managers make decisions on their own, what good are managers? This is a logical question, but the wrong question. Managers are not made managers in order to hold dominion over others. They are managers in order to help do the work the organization needs to get done. Managers — even CEOs — are not pharaohs. This fact is easily lost on those whose thinking has slid into a predictable, self-protecting groove.

The goal of demassification is to create a confederacy of entrepreneurs. You cannot do this if you believe that your employees are a confederacy of dunces. If your employees don't seem to be working on the right things, whose fault is that?

Managers who think only they have the answers have given up on the most basic principle of management — that organizations are made of people, not "units." Managers who think the people below them are incapable of individual decision making are really saying that they themselves are incapable of training, motivating, and explaining. A manager who can work with people, who can work with teams, who can help processes improve and bring out the very best in people, is exactly what a manager should be.

The downside of demassifying. Although there are many risks to centralization, demassifying is not without risk. The biggest risk is doing it wrong. To demassify improperly is to do a great disservice to the work, credentials, and emotions of your employees. And it is easy to go astray by hiring people without the training to handle new responsibilities, by not retraining those who already work for you, by miscommunicating or undercommunicating what is expected, or by throwing demass at them like every other "program of the month."

People are one of the greatest challenges demassifiers face. Under a top-down, centralized management scheme, workers are asked to know their job and to do it, and that's it. In a demassified company, people must be more aware of what their coworkers are doing. Since employees are asked to know things they did not previously need to know, a "knowledge gap" naturally occurs when a system is demassified. Bridging that gap is a problem that managers must solve.

In a demassified workplace, management trusts the intentions and respects the talents of its workers. You don't give people power unless you have confidence that they will be able to handle it. And neither should you give them power without making them accountable for their actions, or without properly training them for the new level of responsibility.

One of the biggest obstacles for companies planning to demassify is overcoming middle management's fear. In a massive corporation, failure or underperformance is easily swept under the carpet. It is generally impossible to blame problems on the individual. In a "street-of-shops" format, though, it's much easier to assign responsibility.

This is a double-edged sword. Though it's great to know who is responsible and accountable for what, it's not great to have a small army of terrified business-unit managers. A demassified corporation must instill a spirit of responsibility for results, but results should not come from browbeating managers, or boiling them in their own juices.

Massification, or centralized management, implies an indifference to the views of employees. "I am the pilot," the massified CEO says, "and the rest of you are just passengers along for the ride." Demass means putting the right information and knowledge at everyone's fingertips, so the entire company can fly in formation.

But in order for line workers to take on a bit of the mantle of independence, they must know a little bit about what everyone else around them is doing. With demassification, people are no longer protected by the tall walls that used to surround each department.

Demass redefines competence. From now on, everyone, whether in engineering, design, marketing, or finance, must be sensitive to the needs of, say, finance (and vice versa), up and down the line. This "cross-functional consciousness," in which everyone knows something about everyone else's job, sounds great in the abstract because it gives team members a stake in the profits and losses their work cranks out. But there is a conspicuous downside: not everyone wants to know how their accomplishments affect profits or losses. Forgivable at perhaps the very lowest level, this "ignorance-is-bliss" attitude can be fatal at the next level — that of the supervisor who thinks he or she has no gift for finance and doesn't want to come to grips with its requirements. "I'm an engineer, not a bookkeeper!" could be the complaint, which could be right, as far as that goes. Except that, in the demassified workplace, workers must be more than just an engineer, or an accountant, or a systems analyst. Within their own business, they must share the responsibility for the "Big Picture."

Eastman Kodak experienced this disparity between job-floor competence and business competence. One of their supervisors reportedly commented: "Hey, we're in great shape down here. I have enough inventory stockpiled here to last us two years and enough extra capacity to do it all in a couple of weeks!" Extra inventory was great for him. But in the new, demassified era, that supervisor must understand that excess inventory is a terrible drag on the business unit's profitability.

Obviously, there has been a gulf of misunderstanding that needs to be breached. It's not enough to sit team managers down, plug in their personal computers for them, and then tell them to figure it out for themselves. Short of actually demassifying, many companies try different approaches to help workers become interested in the larger business vision, including elementals of profit and loss. Some companies make it a little easier with an in-service course on business basics or manufacturing data essentials.

Fortunately, keeping tabs on financial information is much easier on your own networked personal computer than it is on an inaccessible minicomputer- or mainframe-based information system. Demassified information systems have many built-in incentives to learning, instant feedback being the most significant. Managers don't have to wait until the weekend to learn if they are on target; the personal computer throws answers to questions right back at them.

The key to making factory managers better businesspeople, of course, is training. Technical and other nonfinancial people must get over their phobias and reservations about financial data. This requires effective teaching, solid leadership, and a little patience. As the old joke goes, "Education is one of the few things Americans are willing to pay for and not get."[1] We have to move beyond that bit of pessimism, however. Training is the key to a quality work force. But for management to provide good training, it has to see with new, demassified eyes what the education needs are at the independent business-unit level. It means hacking through the thickets of a company's turf jungles and exposing the bureaucratic underbrush to the light of day.

What massification does. Here is an example that epitomizes the kind of destructive turf behaviors that are typical of the massified corporation. It concerns a real, though unidentified company[2] that once, not so long ago, was famous for the rate at which it introduced new products. Month after month this young, compact company rolled out its latest idea, dispatched it to its proper marketing niche, gave it a chance, and if it showed any sign of vitality at all, lent full corporate marketing support to it as a potential money-maker.

In its infancy this company had a distinctly entrepreneurial spirit. When it was small, its leaders knew one another socially as well as professionally, and that spirit trickled down throughout the company. But the company grew. Not too fast or too recklessly; it just grew. And as it added mass, and plants, and new divisions, and new divisions to insert between existing divisions, and mergers and acquisitions to further complicate the original tight corporate model, the rate of new product development began to slow down.

Forty years passed. The first wave of entrepreneurs matured, retired, or just plain lost some of their original spark. And the company began to lose its bearings. It was as if everyone knew what his or her job was, but no one was visionary enough to see the big picture. So they called in outsiders. Here's the company, these outsiders were told; see what you can do to make sense of it.

The outsiders said, oh, you need even more outsiders! Your people haven't accepted that this is a world-class enterprise now. They still long for the old days, when everyone knew everyone. They must be taught the new order of things!

"Professionalism" became the name of the game, which described people who could move interchangeably from business to business, because their professional niche didn't change, no matter what was being manufactured or sold. Act like a major corporation — immense and remote — and the world would treat you like one. That was the idea. Hires at the company were no longer made because "we liked the cut of his jib," as in the old days. Now the central personnel department looked first at an applicant's graduate degrees. As MBAs and people with backgrounds in *Fortune* 500 companies began to flood the company's work force, the company doubled, tripled, and then quadrupled its headcount until it bore zero resemblance to that which the fresh-faced entrepreneurs had started.

With 90,000 employees, it was no longer possible for the CEO to know every vice president on a first-name basis, much less every department head, or every man and woman employed there. Within a 10-year period, this corporation went from 13 new products a year to fewer than two new products every two years. And the rate of future rollouts was estimated at zero, over the next three years. This at a time when its raw marketing and distribution clout was second to none internationally.

Billions in infrastructure, but no creative dynamism! That was what befell this now massive consumer-products company.

The onset of turfism. As management clustered at the center of this corporation — which was decentralized, but on a massive scale — individual work teams, feeling a million light years from meaningful information, clustered together in self-defense. Instead of producing, they blamed. Production was packed with sluggards. Design was loaded with prima donna nitwits. Engineers were all nerds. Finance — let's not even start with finance!

Within their specialized departments, they got along fine. But they didn't know diddly about the unit down the hall, and knew even less about all the other units scattered worldwide. Design teams didn't speak to production teams, and no one spoke to finance.

New ideas foundered in a gridlock of caution and resistance. Trust, which flourished in the old days of bowling leagues and Friday night cocktail parties, withered. Sharing, as a corporate approach to problem solving, likewise ceased to occur. Turfism slowed new product development to a screeching halt.

It was a classic case of corporate disintegration, of what happens at the human level when a company gets too big.

DEMASSIFICATION AND EMPOWERMENT

The successful manager knows something about human nature that the rest do not: that turf attitudes arise not out of something basic and crummy in human nature, but as a response to something perceived to be threatening.

In the case of most turf wars, the feeling of "us against them" usually occurs when the group in question feels an overwhelming need to band together, because they know that they are their only source of strength. They get no support from top management, which doesn't know they exist. They get no support from human resources, which is also centralized and has to appear evenhanded. Production people feel like the water carriers of the business world because they are deliberately excluded from major decisions. And every other department feels exactly the same way.

Demass is primarily about people, and then about information, and finally about power. The link between the three is, however, indisputable. Communication — true communication — is power, and without it, people revert to behaviors that are, if not uncivilized, certainly not what we associate with teamwork and cooperation.

Turf wars are the fault of management, not employees — even if management has no idea they're being waged. But it is usually a crime of omission, not commission. Active, localized leadership creates a healthy atmosphere of collaboration; passive, remote leadership fosters backbiting and malicious compliance.

What to do. In the case of this company, top management had to be made to understand that it cannot possibly know what works best for people at the loading-dock level. When management tries to influence all decisions being made by subordinates, the usual result is that no decisions are made. There is a management axiom: "A great decision never implemented is less useful than an average decision implemented immediately, with gusto."

Fortunately, an internal consultant at the company's international division was given the mandate to "stir things up." This consultant began making recommendations on how to get people working together again and how to get new products rolling out as in the company's gravy days.

The consultant created a solutions team composed of eight line managers and two vice presidents, and met with them several times in a room just off the factory floor. The team met with more than 100 workers, from 11 different departments. One discovery made was that the division had devised an obscure system of approvals whereby no one made a move on any project until the project had been OK'd by no fewer than seven separate department heads. No one could even spend a dime on creating a prototype until that seventh signature appeared on the work order.

It turned out it was no one's fault. Management didn't believe that the number seven was in any way magical. Management saw the sign-off problem as a "trickle-up" rule, something people in the plants devised to cover their tails; the people in the plants assumed the procedure had been handed down to them on stone tablets. Evidently, no one had signed the rule calling for all those signatures!

It was a mind-blowing discovery. It was in no operations manual, not part of any training program. It was like an "urban myth" that sprang up all by itself, in everyone's midst, unaccountably. Seven signatures before anyone could go to the bathroom!

Well, it wasn't really that bad, but it was an example of how encrusted the division had become with fearful habits. Everyone was terrified of doing something wrong and getting blamed — the worst attitude a division dedicated to new product development could have.

Out with the old, in with the new. It was easy to throw out the "seven signatures" procedure since it had never officially existed in the first place. There certainly wasn't any logic behind it. But it took an inquisitive, empowered manager to get at the awful truth.

We are surrounded in manufacturing by a host of "awful truths" every moment we do business. There is not a person who cannot name a dozen serious stupidities that are part and parcel of everyday work life. But pointing a finger at them, naming them, and expunging them requires leadership from above and hard work from below. Lee Iacocca can't inspect every new chassis for dings, but he can let his people know that they will be rewarded for catching mistakes and fixing them, rather than turning the customary blind eye to them and letting them pass through the back door.

Kathy Hudson at Eastman Kodak put it very well: "The challenge today is whether a manager is as able to facilitate in his new role as he was to control in his previous capacity. Today's manager understands that, in a very real sense, he or she works for the team, not the other way around. That is a real switch for lots of people, but it is the absolute truth."

In America, we pay our people the best wages on earth, and they know it. Most of them are talented people and, compared to most of the competition, quite efficient. But we have to let people know it's OK to put their brains to work. The sad truth is that all too often we have encouraged them to switch their brains off. In a competitive world nothing can save us — not even the aura of seven signatures — but ourselves, and our own diligence and creativity.

The upshot to our story? The company went out of the signature business and got back into serious product development. At last count, they were rolling out 25 new products across a two-year cycle — a deluge, compared to its previous stagnation. Many were bombing when they hit the marketplace, but earnings were up because enough products were doing well. And walking from unit to unit, you could see that people had regained the rosy, confident flush of success that had been missing, a feeling that comes from having permission to move from ground zero.

The pain of demassification. Demass is very threatening to people in central information services, as they see their machines moved around, their "society" split up, and its members dispatched to run smaller systems within intimate business groups. Not everyone is equipped to make the transfer. Change is tough. They cannot be blamed if their resistance is very high.

How does a company intent on demassifying handle people who cling to their turf (information services, purchasing, engineering, whatever) as if their very lives depended on it? Organizational psychologists say that eradicating turfism can be pretty easy; you simply change the rules of the game. Where in the past you encouraged turfism by locking people away from one another, you now discourage it by rewarding the formation of effective business units, each of which includes members of every functional specialty. Where your company had once rewarded individual achievement and competition, you now reward teamwork and collaboration. You now institute rewards for sharing, supporting, and helping others succeed. And you make it unmistakably clear to remaining turf warriors that expectations have changed and that turfism will no longer be tolerated.

Some companies use shame techniques, the way a kindergarten teacher might, sending conspicuous turf fighters — usually divisional vice presidents who run their divisions as personal fiefdoms — to stand in the corner, or clean out their desks. It's brutal, it's public, and it gets the message across. Sacrificing a few hard-liners sometimes has a salutary effect on the more mild-mannered infighters. But it can backfire if the punishment creates a backlash of sympathy for the offending party.

I like the idea of rewards better. If positive reinforcement works, then punishment should, except in the most ugly cases, be unnecessary. People want to cooperate; of that I am convinced. Give the cooperative genes a chance to emerge and do their stuff; most individuals will come through splendidly.

Encouraging versatility. It is wrong to demassify by simply passing power down from the top office to the factory floor, then to expect people in the business units to know what to do with it. Power is a means to an end, and to employ it effectively requires distributing information, training, understanding levels of accountability, measuring success, and last, but not least, a high level of flexibility at the business-unit level.

By flexibility I mean that every person in every business unit should understand what his or her fellow team members are doing. A properly demassified business unit in manufacturing operations includes purchasers, accountants, designers, engineers, and production people. A demassified business unit is like a profit-driven company, even though it may number only 100 people.

Tom Peters, in *Thriving on Chaos*, said that people have to learn to embrace change as it engulfs business — that it is the only way to retain a kernel of sanity amid the tumult and to succeed. He extended this advice to managers, but it should be extended to everyone. The old days of the rectangular job description are drawing to a close. We need to acknowledge that a job is much more than what is typed on a scrap of paper. We may be specialists, but we must be generalists as well.

That is the very heart of demassification. There is not a single person in any company who should be oblivious to his or her role in the larger enterprise. There should be a metric that keeps each employee continuously informed of his or her performance and how it has affected company profitability, product or service quality, and customer satisfaction.

An employee is not just an extrusions technician, but a businessperson in the business of meeting customer needs—sure, primarily by running an extrusion machine, but also by keeping an eye open to ways in which his or her business unit can continuously improve. Without this alertness, this flexibility, demass is a sham, just another "program of the month" to bother people who in all likelihood have other things they would rather be doing.

10
The Demassification Dividend

After all is said and done, there is only one important measure of a good business idea — the bottom line. Smart goal setting, organizational revitalization through demassification, and consistent measurement of what a company is trying to manage will improve today's results and give a company the flexibility it will surely need to survive and thrive tomorrow.

Most CEOs with whom I discuss demass invariably steer the conversation around to the topic of bottom-line performance. "How much can I expect demass to add to my profit margins?" they want to know. "And how soon can I expect good things to happen?" These are excellent questions. It does no good to go about all the work of organizationally restructuring a company and downsizing its information-processing systems if the company still winds up losing money and market share.

Demassification will improve a company's performance but it takes time for the benefits to affect a company's bottom line. Everything we know about business reinforces the belief that it is an incremental process by which a solid idea that is well understood, effectively introduced and communicated, and properly executed and managed will prevail, even in the harsh realities of the marketplace.

Entire books were written in the 1980s on the bottom-line blessings that resulted from corporate restructurings that reduced payroll, streamlined command, and achieved synergies of staff and management by merging, acquiring, or wringing a company's neck under threat of Chapter 11. Measuring the success of these restructuring campaigns was relatively easy. You waited a quarter or two, saw how your overall headcount, earnings, and stock prices were changing, and if you liked the numbers, you kept doing whatever you were doing. Demass is a little different. A multibillion dollar company isn't demassified in a day. The actual determination of the success of demassification is a little like the pot of gold at the end of the rainbow; it skitters ahead as you advance toward it. Since demassification is usually undertaken on a unit-by-unit basis and then expanded on a division-by-division basis, its impact on corporate profitability is unlikely to overtake the entire corporation all at once, like a tidal wave.

But progress on strategic fronts within units being demassified can be detected almost immediately, in operational performance metrics such as inventory accuracy, on-time shipments, and product return rates. The effect of these improvements upon the units' profit and loss numbers can be extrapolated across an entire company. And the figures are eye-openers.

In the next few pages, I will present methodology for estimating the potential dollar-and-cents impact of demassification on a single business unit and on a multi-billion-dollar industrial enterprise. To explain this quantification methodology, I borrow heavily from actual case histories, so the numbers you will be reading represent reality rather than academic musings.

QUANTIFYING THE DEMASSIFICATION DIVIDEND AT THE BUSINESS-UNIT LEVEL

Setting the stage. The company being considered is a big one, over $5 billion in sales. It manufactures many different products, but most of them are grouped under five major product divisions. "Toe-in-the-water" demassification was tested in one $10 million business unit that manufactured a single product.

The business unit had a clear mission and was given maximum autonomy to run its own business. Business-unit managers were given responsibility for implementing and operating their own local-area network-based data processing system, with desktop computers on most managers' desks. On their departmental data-processing system they installed a financial and manufacturing resources planning (MRP II) system, sold and serviced by a leading independent software company.

They passed schedules and performance results upward over communication lines to corporate accounting and to other related departments, but they ran their own business. This included handling their own purchasing and order processing, along with handling payables and receivables.

Quantifying your company's performance versus your competition's. Although it seemed impractical for the entire enterprise to get a handle on their comparative overall performance versus similar-sized competitors, it was relatively easy for this single-product business unit, with $10 million in sales, to benchmark itself against its competitors.

The key decision made was to set limits on what to attack. Here is what they did:

- They put a "stake in the ground" and measured where they were at that time in specific performance categories. Then, with outside help, they benchmarked their performance against their best competitors. They then measured the gap between their current performance and where they wanted to be and reset their goals, using their competitors' performance as their yardstick.
- They focused everyone's attention on customer service.
- They established increased profit and cash flow as the two most important quantitative goals.
- They focused on management of receivables and payables for pure cash leverage.
- They focused on inventory reduction for cash plus profit leverage. To reduce inventory they zeroed in on the eight operational activities pivotal to efficient manufacturing. The software package they selected provided special features that allowed careful management of these eight operational activities.
- They committed to begin continuously measuring and tracking (and displaying on big wall charts) their progress against set goals.

Quantifying cash to be mined out of receivables. Controlling receivables is simply a frame of mind. The 38 companies that this unit was benchmarked against averaged from 44 to 79 days of receivables with a median of 54 days.

This business unit was averaging 57 days. Every day of receivables was worth more than $27,000 in cash. They decided there was no reason their receivables should be over 54 days. A 54-day receivables goal was set.

Then, for the first time, they got serious about managing receivables. They used their personal computers to age and track receivables. Periodic meetings were held to review the top-10 overdue accounts. Every morning, collections people screened a complete accounts-receivable report along with a prioritized list of "overdues" on their desktop systems. Unit management reviewed receivables daily on screen in understandable exception charts and graphs. The current status of accounts was displayed in green, yellow, or red numerals, which clearly distinguished those accounts that were OK and those that needed attention.

They reached their goal. Days of receivables went from 57 to 54 in less than three months. Cash that came in the door faster got deposited faster. The benefits tallied up as cash improved by $81,000, with a small but helpful interest bonus of $4,000 on annual profit.

Quantifying cash to be mined out of payables. How soon you pay a payable is controllable. The important thing with managing payables is to have the right goals, be up-front with vendors, and avoid missing promised payment dates. The 38 companies that this unit benchmarked themselves against averaged from 28 to 61 days of payables, with the median being 42 days.

This business unit was making payments to vendors in 30 days. Why so fast? Nobody knew. Each day of payables was worth over $16,000 in cash to them. No one had actually stopped and calculated that amount, either. They decided their payables should be stretched out to at least the 42-day median of their competitors. The 42-day goal was set.

Before, payables had been processed on a schedule that mostly had to do with convenience. Now the unit was starting to understand the cash impact of managing payables. They worked with their vendors to renegotiate terms, keeping payables as long as practical but always with a minimum 42- to 45-day target goal in mind. They continued to take all attractive discounts and faithfully paid when promised, but no earlier.

Every morning, on their desktop computer screens, accounting accessed a complete accounts-payable report that displayed the last date payments could be made along with a special "Why did we pay so soon?" analysis of each early payment. It became clear that the key to maintaining payables to a targeted level was to keep your promises *but not to pay one day earlier*.

Unit management, using their personal computers, reviewed payables by looking at exception charts and graphs. The current status of accounts was presented in green, yellow, or flashing red, making it clear what was being paid early and why.

They reached their goal. Payables stretched out from 30 to 42 days in less than five months. The quantified benefits were cash improved by $199,000, along with an earned interest bonus of $10,000.

Quantifying the multiple payoffs of improving manufacturing operations. The primary reason inventory gets out of control in any company is because of a breakdown in people-to-people communications. Communication breakdowns result in lack of trust. If you can't trust the other person, or the other department, you start building buffers to protect yourself. These buffers often come in the form of too much inventory. Some people call this "just-in-case" inventory.

My intent here is neither to launch into a tirade about the evils of too much inventory and why it happens nor to tell you about all the exciting new theories and techniques on how to minimize bad inventory. Most reputable computer-based, manufacturing resource planning software systems, fed accurate data and attended by reasonably competent people, should help any company manufacture more efficiently. Still, this computer-savvy business unit, which had been forced to use an MIS-mandated mainframe manufacturing system for years, continued to encounter the nagging problem of too much inventory.

The business unit was averaging 106 days of inventory. However, the 38 companies that this unit was benchmarked against averaged much better, 40 to 99 days of inventory, with the median being 62 days. Each day of inventory was worth over $16,000 to the unit. But, unlike payables and receivables, where they felt confident about improving performance, they had already tried about everything they could think of to reduce inventory, but so far hadn't seen much improvement.

The principal reason they selected the manufacturing software package they used was that it represented commercial-strength, productized "best-in-class business practices," which stressed management of eight operational activities that are critical to efficient manufacturing. Years of factory-floor experience indicate that these activities are pivotal to customer service, reducing inventory, improving quality, and lowering operating costs.

These eight activities (expressed in greater detail in the Appendix), are:

- Inventory accuracy
- Bill-of-material accuracy
- Item responsibilities assigned
- Lead times assigned
- Standards costs assigned
- Practical schedules planned
- Released orders scheduled when needed
- Planned shipments not past due

It is possible to summarize these eight pivotal activities into a single readout using a type of a digital thermometer, formally referred to as "probable systems communication." Digital thermometers need numeric scales. So, an equation was established so that this "probable systems communication" readout could be quantified as a percentage — where 0 percent means absolutely terrible communications (i.e., terrible business health), and a 100 percent readout indicates near-perfect intrabusiness unit system communication. This overarching statistic therefore summarizes all eight measurements into one useful number so that any business can see at a glance when it is getting progressively healthier or sicker.

The profit-related outcomes from improving the eight activities are expressed in four easily understood resultants — on-time shipment performance, inventory turn performance, cost of goods sold, and operating expenses. These four performance factors synergistically build on each other. On-time shipment significantly improves inventory turns, and faster inventory turns translate into lower cost of goods sold and lower operating expenses — a fiscal chain reaction.

Let's now go through the numbers using these eight pivotal manufacturing activities as a roadmap to increased profitability. This was the business unit's level of performance at the beginning of the measured period, their stake in the ground:

Stake in the Ground

	Months					
	1	2	3	4	5	6
Eight Operational Activities						
Inventory accuracy	94%	—	—	—	—	—
Bill of material accuracy	91%	—	—	—	—	—
Item responsibility assigned	92%	—	—	—	—	—
Lead times assigned	92%	—	—	—	—	—
Standard costs assigned	87%	—	—	—	—	—
Practical schedules planned	22%	—	—	—	—	—
Released orders scheduled for the future	53%	—	—	—	—	—
Released orders, no shortages	25%	—	—	—	—	—
Probable System Communication						
Calculated, operational activities accuracy (accuracy percentages multiplied times themselves)	2%	—	—	—	—	—
Resultant Outcomes						
On-time shipment performance	20%	—	—	—	—	—
Inventory turn performance						
expressed in turns	3.4	—	—	—	—	—
expressed in days	106.0	—	—	—	—	—
Cost of goods sold as percent of sales	66%	—	—	—	—	—
Operating expenses as percent of sales	30%	—	—	—	—	—

There were several interesting side notes about this business unit's operational activities. They didn't seem to be operating too poorly except in the last three or four operational activities; the top four operational activities were all above the 90 percent achievement level. Therefore, they quickly decided to focus on improving their performance in the bottom three operational activities.

"Probable system communication" (which I have characterized as a digital thermometer) was a major new concept for this newly empowered business unit to grasp and take to heart.

Unfortunately, communication errors have a multiplier effect as they reverberate through any group of workers trying to do a complicated job in unison. Therefore it was decided, using reasonably sound mathematical logic, that this reverberation effect could be assigned a metric value by simply multiplying the "accuracy percentage" of each of the eight operational activities times one another.

The percentage assigned to probable system communication for this business unit, at its present performance level, was therefore 2 percent (e.g., the product of multiplying 94 percent times 91 percent — all the way through to the final, times 25 percent, which results in a percentage with a lot of insignificant digits but rounds off to 2 percent).

This numerical indicator of the quality of good communication may not seem perfect, but in my experience its trend line over time always turns out to have very close correlation to actual bottom-line performance trend lines. When it rises, performance goes up, and vice versa.

The calculated probable system communication for this business unit was a low 2 percent. No wonder communication was so terrible before it was demassified! No wonder their actual measured performance in two vitally important "resultant outcomes" was only 20 percent on-time shipments to customers, and a dismal 3.4 (though better than companywide) inventory turns a year! No wonder they were losing ground to competition.

As a cohesive team working together, they zeroed in on the three operational activities where their performance had been poor. The following is the same chart as presented previously, but this time the chart also reflects the business unit's performance for five subsequent months after they had placed their stake in the ground. With their transformed attitudes and through using their own internally controlled manufacturing support system, they succeeded at incrementally improving, month by month, their performance in all the operational activities being measured.

Performance Over 6 Months

	Months					
	1	2	3	4	5	6
Eight Operational Activities						
Inventory accuracy	94%	94%	94%	94%	94%	94%
Bill of material accuracy	91%	90%	91%	91%	92%	91%
Item responsibility assigned	92%	95%	98%	99%	93%	99%
Lead times assigned	92%	92%	95%	98%	98%	98%
Standard costs assigned	87%	93%	96%	96%	97%	97%
Practical schedules planned	22%	80%	91%	95%	95%	95%
Released orders scheduled for the future	53%	82%	97%	93%	96%	95%
Released orders, no shortages	25%	90%	95%	94%	98%	97%
Probable System Communication						
Calculated, operational activities accuracy (accuracy percentages multiplied times themselves)	2%	41%	64%	66%	72%	70%
Resultant Outcomes						
On-time shipment performance	20%	21%	29%	38%	54%	65%
Inventory turn performance						
expressed in turns	3.4	3.7	4.4	5.1	5.4	5.9
expressed in days	106.0	99.0	83.0	72.0	68.0	62.0
Cost of goods sold as percent of sales	66%	66%	64%	63%	62%	62%
Operating expenses as percent of sales	30%	29%	29%	28%	28%	28%

As performance in the eight (and especially in the last three) operational activities steadily improved, the "probable system communication" measurement increased. The thermometer rose. As this indicator increased month after month, so did unit performance.

On-time shipment performance to customers improved to 65 percent. The goal for this should always be 100 percent, but all in all not a bad improvement over the six-month period. Inventory turns improved dramatically. This would be worth big bucks to any company, because financing standing inventory and carrying excess inventory is expensive. Cost of goods sold and operating expenses as percentages of sales also showed improvement.

The demassification dividend at the business-unit level. The chart on the next page summarizes this business unit's improvement in profit and cash. Only three improvement categories are quantified — inventory, receivables, and payables. An annual sales growth rate of 15 percent was built into this chart to show how operating improvements, once implemented, continued to improve profit and cash over time.

QUANTIFYING THE DEMASSIFICATION DIVIDEND AT THE ENTERPRISE LEVEL

Setting the stage. Thus, we have quantified the demassification dividend achieved by a single business unit within one division of a $5 billion enterprise. The company ran five major product divisions. After witnessing the financial impact of demassifying one tough-to-fix business unit, the company's

Performance Improvements: Impact on Profit and Cash
(assuming a 15% growth rate; in millions)

Days of inventory if decreased from 106 to 62 days:

	Current	Year 2	Year 3	Year 4	Year 5
Improved profit	$0.182	$0.209	$0.240	$0.276	$0.317
Conserved cash	$0.727	$0.109	$0.125	$0.144	$0.166

Days of receivables if decreased from 57 to 54 days:

	Current	Year 2	Year 3	Year 4	Year 5
Improved profit	$0.004	$0.005	$0.005	$0.006	$0.007
Conserved cash	$0.081	$0.012	$0.014	$0.016	$0.018

Days of payables if decreased from 30 to 42 days:

	Current	Year 2	Year 3	Year 4	Year 5
Improved profit	$0.010	$0.011	$0.013	$0.015	$0.018
Conserved cash	$0.199	$0.030	$0.035	$0.040	$0.046

Improved performance if above improvements are realized:

	Current	Year 2	Year 3	Year 4	Year 5
Improved profit	$0.196	$0.225	$0.258	$0.297	$0.342
Conserved cash	$1.007	$0.151	$0.174	$0.200	$0.230

top management agreed to set up a small senior-management task force to review a methodology for quantifying the potential savings of demassifying the entire $5 billion corporation.

The resultant report presented to the senior management task force was an eye-opener. It showed how significantly financial performance could rise, if a large company could become light on its feet and commit to match smaller competitors' flexibility. The methodology used in preparing the task force report may help readers assess the potential for performance gains with demassification.

Quantifying the value of improving manufacturing operations. Large companies claim and often believe that sheer size makes doing business less expensive. Buying in volume, vertical integration, and corporate synergies all supposedly make them cost competitive. I believe, however, that these advantages, while devoutly to be wished, are harder to find in reality than in books.

Small companies nearly always have higher inventory turns than their large counterparts. Small companies also have faster receivables turnaround. They get products to market faster. This superior efficiency is reflected in stock prices, where higher price-to-earnings ratios suggest that smaller companies are being given credit on Wall Street for getting more bang for their bucks.

Here's the methodology I use to pinpoint what smaller competitors' actual performance is and how to quantify what it would mean to a large company to match smaller competitors' operating efficiencies. I used this methodology to prepare a report for the senior management task force.

I took a copy of the $5 billion enterprise's annual report, and then consulted the latest edition of Robert Morris Associates' Annual Statement Studies. Robert Morris Associates (RMA) is the national association of bank loan and credit officers, and the book is an annual avalanche of definitive financial data on virtually every kind of business, comparing financial information of companies with total assets of less than $100 million. It offers extensive information on earnings, sales, expenses, inventory turns, and other factors by industry segment. With the RMA book in hand, I listed the company's major lines of business and the percentage of company revenues and earnings each was responsible for. This was the profile drawn from the enterprise's published annual report:

Enterprise's Lines of Business

Financial Data	% of Revenues	% of Earnings
Electrical products	31	41
Electrical power equipment	14	13
Tools and hardware	17	15
Automotive products	17	15
Petroleum and industrial equipment	21	16

Using the RMA information, I determined how many companies in each business line were profiled in the Annual Statement Studies — 130 companies in electrical products and power equipment, 130 in tools and hardware, 220 in automotive products, and 30 in petroleum and industrial equipment.

Each business line was indexed by a number, called the SIC (Standard Industrial Classification) number. Translating each of the enterprise's five lines of business (e.g., tools and hardware) into RMA's nearest equivalent ("cutlery, handtools, and general hardware" — SIC Nos. 3421, 3423, 3425 and 3429) seemed a bit arbitrary at times. But it was close enough for my purposes. Best of all, the sample was large, ensuring that the comparison would be meaningful. Next, I created the following chart, which recaps the company's financial data:

Enterprise's Financial Profile

Financial Data	$ Billions
Sales	5.200
Cost of sales	3.500
Expenses (selling, administrative costs, interest, etc.)	1.200
Cash and other	0.028
Accounts receivable	1.100
Inventory and other	1.700
Fixed assets (plants, property, equipment less depreciation)	1.600

Next, I compared the enterprise's financial performance to the host of smaller competitors in each line of business. I had to cross-reference each business line with the respective tables of data in the RMA book. I focused on two key operations categories — the RMA statistics for inventory turns and receivables turnaround. (This is a subset of the categories used previously to study the small business unit.)

By dividing cost of sales ($3.5 billion) by inventory ($1.7 billion), I learned that the company's current composite inventory turn figure was 2.06. According to RMA, median inventory turn level for the composite of small companies in the same business lines as the $5 billion company was 3.9, meaning that half of these small companies were doing even better. Even the worst of these little companies appeared to be doing better. No big surprise here — everyone expects small companies to be more efficient with inventory.

Now, if our large company could speed up its overall inventory turns, from 2.06 to 3.90 turns, to equal the small companies' inventory turns, what would be the potential improvement in financial performance, assuming nothing else changed?

Enterprise's Potential Financial Performance	
New Financial Data	**Performance**
Cost of sales (doesn't change)	$3.500 billion
New inventory turns (increased to)	3.9 turns
New inventory value (goes down to)	$0.900 billion
An inventory reduction of	$0.800 billion

Two big financial benefits would accompany this level of inventory reduction:

- Assets (cash) invested in inventory would, over time, be reduced by $800 million.
- Carrying costs on inventory (i.e., warehousing, spoilage, theft, handling, etc.) would be reduced by about $200 million in ongoing expenses annually, assuming normal inventory carrying costs of 25 percent.

These are significant numbers! If "smallness" isn't the reason all these smaller companies are outperforming massive companies, what is?

Quantifying the value of managing receivables. Using the RMA again, I saw that the median for days of receivables for smaller companies (averaged out according to the five product divisions) was 55 days. The enterprise's sales figure was $5.1 billion, and accounts receivables totaled $1.1 billion. By dividing sales by 365 (days of the year), I roughly figured daily sales of about $14 million. By dividing the enterprise's $1.1 billion of accounts receivable by daily sales, I arrived at the figure of approximately 78 current days of receivables — a long time. If the big enterprise could somehow achieve a decrease of 23 days from that (thus matching the 55-day average figure of smaller companies), what would be their benefit in terms of cash flow? I multiplied $14 million per day by 23, and had the answer — $322 million. That's a lot of money in the eyes of any corporate treasurer.

How cost reductions affect stock value. Now comes the part that really got the attention of the senior-management task force at this $5 billion enterprise. Was there a way to translate demass-driven factory-floor productivity gains into measurable shareholder benefit? Indeed there was, because sustainable changes in any large company's quarterly cash flow and earnings eventually attracts Wall Street's attention.

In this case, the realistic potential benefits from demassification were an annual inventory expense savings of $200 million and $800 million reduction in cash tied up in inventory. Additionally, there was a receivables cash receipts speedup of $322 million.

Here is the company's potential stock price impact, excluding any consideration of imputed interest on incremental cash:

Enterprise's Potential Stock Performance

Financial Data	"Actual" Before Demassification (in dollars)	"Potential" After Demassification (in dollars)
Before tax profit	475 million	675 million
Earnings per share	4.40	6.25
Current stock price	30.00	43.00*

* Holding constant Enterprise's current price/earnings multiple, which at the time of this study was a low 6.8

Needless to say, a potential stock price improvement of $30 to $43 represented a significant opportunity to shareholders.

Summing up. The intent of this chapter has been to show how quantifying the demassification dividend is possible. Within a single business unit you can not only estimate what the dividend should be, but you can also quickly demonstrate the substance behind these estimates.

For a massive corporation, about the best we can do is broadly estimate what can be achieved by "powering down" a massive organization; putting inventory and receivables and payables, and the information-processing tools to manage them, into the hands of people who can actually affect profit and loss. Then, top management must decide whether and when to proceed down the path toward total corporate demassification.

Money can and should be saved, and made, by reorganizing a big company so that it can act like a small one. That money, along with a higher stock price, is the "demassification dividend."

Epilog The Water Is Fine

Companies and their managements do not improve by doing the comfortable thing. They progress by facing challenges squarely and adapting to them as they would to an approaching wave. A big wave is drawing near to American business. The choice is clear: learn to surf (demassify) or prepare to wipe out.

Though I was raised in Missouri, I have spent a good portion of my adult life in Texas. A lot of pride and a lot of wisdom can be found in both states. When I lived in Austin, Texas, I had a neighbor who loved to brag about the bigness of Texas. This neighbor was once chatting with a down-to-earth friend of mine from Oran, Missouri, who was visiting my wife and me over the weekend. "You know," my neighbor said, "on my ranch up on the Pecos, I can hop in my truck and drive all day and never reach the property line."

"Yes, I know exactly what you mean," replied the Missourian, "I had a truck just like that once myself."

The truth is, America has always been profoundly ambivalent about the virtues of bigness. We are a large country made up of small states — we fought a war over the issue of, among other things, centralization. We say we like to stick up for the little guy — yet we glory in all things oversized, from the Grand Canyon and the Great Lakes to the Astrodome and AT&T.

Our entire political dialogue for the past century can be summed up as an argument over whether government should be big, centralized, and involved in everything, or small, scattered, and discreet. We admire the entrepreneur, but we worship the tycoon. The "big business hater" wants to break up the supercompanies into less oppressive components; the "big business lover" extols the virtues of economies of scale, synergy, and vertical integration.

I believe that this ambivalence is part of the American genius, that neither big nor small is necessarily good or bad and that each has its purposes and advantages. No one who looks seriously at the threats we face from competition abroad, from companies the size of Matsushita, Fujitsu, and Toyota, would conclude that the answer lies in breaking U.S. *Fortune* 500 manufacturing companies into so many machine shops. The best way to take 1,000 passengers around the world in style is probably not to set them afloat in four-passenger rowboats.[1]

Like it or not, big is with us for the duration; we need it to compete. But the catch is that we also need the flexibility and adaptability intrinsic to smaller enterprises. Getting bigger is every business's goal — *yet bigness is bad for business.*

That's the Catch-22.

THE CHALLENGE FROM ABROAD

The Japanese are also ambivalent about size, but in a different way. They say, "It is hard for a large man to fully exercise his wits."[2] The Japanese must surely look at our bloated megacorporations, even those with traditions of excellence, such as IBM, and see them as doomed by the organizational fat that encompasses them.

The beauty of Japanese management philosophy is that size — the historic be-all and end-all for the imperial U.S. corporation — isn't what counts; process efficiency counts. From their earliest post–World War II experiences, the Japanese have diligently kept their eye on the processes that have been the living cells of even their largest corporations today. The Japanese have not needed to demassify organizationally because, intellectually, they have focused on the little things that matter in the world of business.

Japan's astounding success has derived in part from their genius for focusing on internal business processes, and, to some extent, from their determination to meet customers' needs quickly. Though Japan's industrial core is highly centralized and in many ways insensitive and autocratic, their organizational dynamics are very different from those of large American companies.

In Japan, giant computers are not central to business to the degree they are in America. Gains the Japanese have made in terms of productivity, reduction in waste, improvement in quality and their incredible ability to delight customers with ingenious and marketable product variations have come through small group-driven operations improvements.

When the Japanese begin to seriously apply computerization to scheduling and operations management — as they will in less than five years — they will again jump forward with additional cost, quality, and time-to-market gains.

While we are working to improve ourselves, they will be working to improve themselves, too. Look for Japan to further increase production flexibility, to hold its own competitively, no matter what the yen does on international exchanges, and to become ever swifter at developing and rolling out new products that coincide with customer needs.

Because it has more money to spend and because it believes in long-term approaches, Japan significantly outspends the U.S. on research and development, and the gulf between the two is growing. U.S. research and development costs as a percent of gross national product have hovered around 1.8 percent for the past decade. Japan's has risen to 3 percent — doubling itself — over that period.[3]

In addition, the Japanese appear to have a different attitude about leadership. The traditional model for the CEO in American business is the conquistador, the take-no-prisoners strongman. Japan has its share of autocrats, but a more typical role is leader-as-servant, an individual responsible for facilitating the success of the whole team, i.e., the company. Since the leader is servant, it is sometimes difficult to tell whether power trickles down or up. It is one of the many ways in which American organizations are hard put to learn from Japan — we haven't the cultural underpinnings to emulate the Japanese model.

It is said that Japan has a talent for teamwork, whereas Americans have a propensity for individual effort. John Fucini, in *Working for the Japanese*, made clear, using his experiences as a manager at a Honda transplant factory in California, how irreconcilable certain Japanese practices were with ours.[4]

For years, Fucini said, we laughed at the Japanese, partly out of our own sense of cultural superiority, partly out of our awareness of just how far they had sunk in the aftermath of World War II. So great was our sense of global and historic primacy that, by the early 1970s, intellectuals in this country were contending that, in a sense, history was over — there were no economic worlds left to conquer.

The Japanese made quick work of that fallacy. Their versions of capitalism, of labor relations, and of participatory management bore little resemblance to anything we had on the boards.

The latest wrinkle is Japan's willingness to poke fun at U.S. work practices. Japanese politicians such as lawmaker Yoshio Sakurauchi blamed the $41 billion trade surplus on "the deterioration in the quality of U.S. workers." Such remarks indicate a growing Japanese sentiment that our workers are lazy, uneducated, unmotivated.

These accusations are not true, not exactly. American workers are more productive than their Japanese counterparts, although we do have more leisure time. American workers are light years from the 30 percent illiteracy figure Prime Minister Miyazawa quoted in his celebrated remark — though it is true that, as free consumers, we pick and choose what we wish to learn. American workers have plenty of motivation — though perhaps it is mismotivation; perhaps we are motivated more by personal gain and less by the challenges of excellence or team achievement.

James Fallows, a commentator who has spent much of his professional life living in Japan and other parts of the Far East, speaks knowingly of our "discovery" of Japan:

> When Americans did give Japan the attention it deserved, I thought they went overboard, seeing it not just as a formidable challenger but as a repository of the values America had to reclaim. Japanese managers planned for the long term, Japanese disputes were solved by consensus rather than lawsuits, Japanese students studied more, Japanese families saved more, even Japanese criminals confined themselves to small-potatoes crimes. Japan

> had planning, discipline, order; America needed more of the same things.[5]

Here was competition, and plenty of it. The Japanese had, it seemed, powers of industrial concentration that made us appear hopelessly shortsighted and indifferent about the key issues of quality, flexibility, and customer satisfaction.

America's fate. The question isn't, Will the United States continue as a manufacturing power? Manufacturing, contrary to fuzzy notions of a "post-industrial economy," will continue to be the bedrock of the American economy, no matter how much consulting we do and no matter how many insurance policies we sell.[6]

It seems to me that the question is, What kind of manufacturer will we be: a low-end responder or a high-end innovator? Will we be makers of low-margin components or high-margin end-products? Will we be followers or leaders? Demass approximates some of the effects of Japan's leader-as-servant model. It makes the manager less a controller and more of an orchestrator, while it puts real power in the hands of those who know best how to use it — the people working at the business-unit level.

Demass accepts the idea of size, even while it attacks the problems associated with it — stalled communications, inflexibility, and an indifference to the "little things" that, in Japan, stand as the foundation for its industrial might.

Peter Drucker has written about what the future holds for manufacturing. He says that three points, paraphrased here,[7] will distinguish the "factory of 1999":

- *Quality*. Statistical quality control, begat of the tools of Walter Shewhart and W. Edwards Deming, and enhanced by the Japanese theory of continuous improvement (*kaizen*) will be the global religion of manufacturers.

- *Business-mindedness.* Manufacturing accounting practices of the next century will transform all production decisions into business decisions — a world of difference from the old hidebound cost accounting that was instituted in the 1920s.
- *Demassification.* Ford didn't build a system at River Rouge, Drucker says — he built a monster, an "assembly planet." The day of the massive plant is done, and the dawn of demassification (my term, not Drucker's) is at hand. Say good-bye to the factory as battleship; say hello to manufacturing as a "flotilla" of autonomous business units.

Demassification, American-style, offers numerous, almost irresistible competitive advantages. Most noticeably, it's cheap. Revamping information systems and junking mainframes may fill up our technology landfills, but the immediate bottom-line results are attractive even to those most enamored of "Big Information."

In addition, in an age of empowerment and participation, the technology downsizing that goes with demassification results in an ease of use that tends to bring everyone into the act. Virtually everyone can be trained to use a personal computer, and virtually everyone prefers the user-friendly interface and interactive dynamics to the remote and inflexible ponderings of yesterday's big systems.

It sounds so simple: a system that is usable will be used. Mistakes no one knew how to report can now be reported. Details that could not be called to attention before can now be attended to.

THE TRANSFORMING POWER OF DEMASS

The central thrust of demass is organizationally transforming a monolithic corporation into a street of shops — an assortment of efficient, self-managed business units.

Eastman Kodak was the first company to put words to and then adopt the "street-of-shops" vision. For Kodak, the "street" was a literal one, with so much of its manufacturing done along miles of corridors under a single roof in the Apparatus Division outside Rochester, New York. But the real "street" is the avenue that runs through each corporation's organizational chart.

Conventional charts show central management as the source and dispenser of strategy and divisions as respectful implementers. Individual departments, where the actual work must occur, are left off the chart completely. The process for decision making in these companies is easy to understand but impossibly difficult to speed up.

Demassified companies' organization charts are less tidy — more dynamic. Usually they can't even be kept current. Within overall mission guidelines, business units are expected to plot their own courses, find their own markets, speed their own products to market, and operate via processes that work best for them. Winning races becomes mandatory; how to trim the sails, optional.

People's outlook and sense of belonging is different in a demassified work environment. Everyone is not only allowed but also expected to contribute. Become a part of the team or you'll hurt the team. There is an understandable linkage between assembly line performance and the business unit's financial and quality performance.

There is no hiding behind the bureaucracy, no place for "seven signatures" to survive. Customers, both external and internal, are so close that you deal with them every day. When your customers are mad you know why. When they are delighted with your products and services you know who is responsible.

With demass, the workplace is small, intimate, and manageable. People work in teams on an almost familial basis. The sense of being a cog in an oversized machine is gone and replaced with the sense of being a vital part of a compact, efficient group. In this workplace people are empowered to do what they know is right and to deliver the best possible work to the next team.

This is the look and feel of demass, of the "street of shops"; but what does it actually deliver in terms of making companies more competitive and the country stronger?

First and perhaps most important, demass delivers flexibility. Large organizations take years to change. Small business units can turn on a dime. Products and services are produced faster, better, and more profitably. New products get out the door faster.

Demass delivers experience-rooted career development. In a massive organization one individual makes executive decisions governing the actions of tens of thousands. In a demassified company there are hundreds of companies, each with its own chief operating officer. Each business unit is a mangement testing ground that provides the corporation with a wealth of "draft choices" to consider for advancement. This breadth of management opportunities can help shatter the "glass ceiling" that has kept talented women and minorities in large corporations from the career development opportunities they deserve — and the organization needs.

Demass strengthens accountability. Massive organizations have so much data from so many places on so many activities that it is impenetrable. The corporate woodwork is riddled with waste and inactivity. Individual bad work is undetectable. In a "street of shops" there is nowhere to hide. Managers know who is doing great work and who is just getting by. Managers can step in early and get the lagging employee back on track before the work and the employee's future suffer irreparable damage. Whatever top managers may think they will be giving up in ability to consolidate all the numbers, they will more than make up in overall accountability.

Demass will add jobs — profit-generating jobs. Over the past 30 years employment growth at our largest corporations has been flat. Employment growth in the United States since the 1960s has taken place in small companies. It is clear to those who will objectively reason why. Small companies grow and become profitable or die, and when they die others spring up to replace them. Massive companies stagnate.

WHY WE WAIT

If demass is so great, why aren't more companies doing it? Good question. I take some solace in the quotation of that wily old strategist, Niccolò Machiavelli: "There is nothing more difficult to take in hand," he wrote, "more perilous to conduct, or more uncertain in its success, than to take the lead in the introduction of a new order of things." More to the point, perhaps, might be George Hannye's observation: "Once you've spent hundreds and millions of dollars creating a strong MIS center, it seems like a shame to throw it away."

By tracking management trends, restructurings, and other news from *Fortune* 500 companies, I have compiled data suggesting that fewer than 15 percent of major U.S. industrial corporations are in any way pursuing radically decentralized organizational restructuring with lockstepped information-systems downsizing. Why so few?

To begin with, Machiavelli knew what he was talking about. Human nature, while malleable, is not made of Spandex and does not seek out opportunities for radical transformation. Even when people need desperately to change, it is not always possible for them to do so.

My experience, for instance, has been that managers can put up with an almost totally intolerable status quo, *if* they are able to hold onto their informal manual controls. If they have this single lifeline to practical sanity, under their sole control, they can put up with an awful lot of nonsense — overscheduling, underscheduling, feast-or-famine order booking, a whirlwind of conflicting priorities, and the ubiquitous, get-it-out-the-door, end-of-period, drop-that, do-this, forget-what-I-just-told-you panic.

Lots of manufacturers are waiting for government to help. Some hope for an industrial policy; others hope for a handout; a lot of them are waiting for a large dose of protectionism to help them buy time to compete. But if they are waiting for Congress to get on the stick, they have a long wait in store for them.

Pollster Peter Hart has conducted surveys of the knowledge base of members of Congress, and the results were dismaying — our elected representatives are sorely unaware of manufacturing's productivity improvements, its export growth, or its technological advances. As a result, Congress is not likely to suddenly sit up and make an informed decision. Speaking of Congress and government in general, demassification is an idea they should ponder. But that is another, and a forlorn, story. Meanwhile, government help? Forget about it. Bureaucracy adds to inertia. Bureaucracy would rather we not do something wrong than do something right.

The distance between a line manager on the shop floor in Pennsylvania and decision makers on the top floor in New York is growing, despite all the management fads that have come along. It is not getting easier for the little guy to be heard — it is getting harder.

Across the vast gulf of size and distance, good ideas get lost. And manufacturing products is a cautious business — we are much more adept at applying a Band-Aid to a festering wound than plotting ways to avoid future cuts.

Then there is good old *analysis paralysis.* Was anyone ever fired for saying, "Let's study it some more?" Indeed, why rush into things? The state of technology, like a mountain stream, changes with each passing second. Management can't be expected to stay on top of every innovation. And how is an executive or manager supposed to know that exact moment, that window of opportunity, when a new technology passes from the to-be-avoided status of *pioneering*, to the riveting status of *essential to maintain our competitive edge*?

If we change today, we'll still have to change again tomorrow. So why change today? Maybe we should save up all our changes until we're in a change mood. Evolution by procrastination!

Finally, there is the sticky matter of balancing perceived cost with perceived risk. Even great bargains aren't free.

Demass is the *what*; organizational restructuring and information-processing technology downsizing are the *how*.

What will America do? I see us poised, as on a high-diving board, and far below is the ocean we must dive into. How can we do it? No one is born to high dive — even an infant is endowed with depth perception to guard against this very sort of eventuality. Our knees knock, our teeth chatter — how can we possibly take the plunge?

Yet dive we must.

The world of business and manufacturing is full of competent, experienced, thoughtful people. Most people are eager to do their jobs right. But they can't go where they need to go without first getting top management's go-ahead. And top management just isn't sure what to do. We need to break away from our old mind-sets about what works and what doesn't. We need to stop being afraid of our own workers, and start to trust them. We need to join with them in pursuing the common goal of competitive excellence. They are up for it! We need to admit, finally, that something is broken and that it needs fixing.

Some forward-thinking CEOs foresee, as I do, a new dawn, a demassified era in which people are allowed to be rational, where people do things right because they want to. Because it excites them. Because quality and excellence are passions. Because their good ideas are being put to the test of reality, and when they work, they become part of the process.

We who manufacture are not like other people. Other people *do* things, but we *make* things. Now is the time to do a lot of *making*. Making up for lost time. Making our own companies see the light of day, and leading them through the change processes. Making a difference in the way our country competes in the reforming world economy.

Demassification will be a new way to manage your company. It represents change, but it embodies leadership principles that worked yesterday and that will work tomorrow: respect for the individual, personal responsibility and accountability, and understood and shared goals. Launching it within your company may be frightful to contemplate, but so is continuing in the safety of current habits, and steadily losing ground.

Surf's up. You can either ride the wild wave, or be engulfed by it. I say, *go*. Embrace, don't fear, the need for rapid and continuous change. Enable your company to respond to the turmoil enveloping it, and it will gain an insuperable competitive advantage.

Appendix
Eight Measures Pivotal to Efficient Manufacturing

Inventory Accuracy

Inventory accuracy is essential to plan and control the factory, to build on schedule and achieve the desired customer service level in the most efficient way. Inaccurate inventory balances cause stockouts, which interrupt production schedules, delay orders, and increase work-in-progress (WIP) inventories.

Bill-of-Material Accuracy

Bill-of-material accuracy also is essential to build and ship products on schedule. Inaccurate bills cause delays in schedules while the correct parts are expedited to the delayed order. Delays result in excess work-in-process inventory and excessive inventories of the wrong parts — parts that get planned but aren't needed.

Item Responsibilities Assigned

Someone must be responsible for planning, ordering, and controlling every item. Unless responsibilities are assigned, there will be items that everybody thinks somebody else is watching. These "orphaned" items will eventually create stock shortages.

Lead Times Assigned

Lead times are used to plan order placement so that items are received and available for use precisely when the production schedule calls for them. Too much lead time bloats inventory. Unassigned lead times and lead times that are too short cause shortages, production delays, and excessive WIP inventory.

Standard Costs Assigned

Accurate standard costs need to be assigned to every item so that proper attention and priority is placed on planning and reordering each item. Standard costs are also required to value the inventory for financial reporting.

Practical Schedules Planned

Many factors are considered when developing the production schedules, and it's impossible to manually determine how all the planning factors will interact to support your production schedules and inventory plans.

Released Orders Scheduled When Needed

When manufacturing and purchase orders are not completed on time and as required, they "clog" the factory with unknown resource and component requirements. Priorities assigned to past-due orders lose all meaning. Orders not scheduled to be completed as required will cause others to be delayed. The result is excessive WIP and lengthened lead times. Before long, nothing can be completed on time.

Planned Shipments Not Past Due

MRP II systems are driven by customer demand. Whether you are build-to-order, assemble-to-order, or make-to-stock, in the end all manufacturers are driven by customer orders. To the extent that past-due customer shipments are not rescheduled to future dates, the MRP II planning engine is forced to begin with inaccurate data, which yields an inaccurate plan.

Notes

CHAPTER 1

1. World Economic Forum and IMD International. *World Competitiveness Report*, Lausanne, 10th, 11th, and 12th eds., 1990, 1991, and 1992.
2. Michael A. Verespej, "Sidney Harman's Message: We Need More Manufacturers, Not Pretenders," *Industry Week*, February 6, 1989, pp. 16-18.
3. David Halberstam, *The Reckoning* (New York: William Morrow, 1986), p. 222.
4. Dana Milbank, "Dying Breed: No Glamour, No Glory, Being a Manufacturer Today Can Take Guts." *Wall Street Journal*, June 3, 1991, p. 1.
5. Lois Therrien, "The Upstarts Teaching McDonalds a Thing or Two," *Business Week*, October 21, 1991, p. 122.
6. Richard Schonberger, *Building a Chain of Customers* (New York: Free Press, 1989).

CHAPTER 2

1. John Leslie King, "Centralized versus Decentralized Computing," *Computing Surveys*, Vol. 15, No. 4, December 1983.

2. Paul Kennedy, *The Rise and Fall of the Great Powers* (New York: Random House 1987), p. 23.
3. David Halberstam, *The Reckoning* (New York: William Morrow, 1986), pp. 105-106.
4. *The Economist*, "Centralising Again" (Editorial), August 13, 1988.
5. Albert Lee, *Call Me Roger: The Story of How Roger Smith, Chairman of General Motors, Transformed the Industrial Leader into a Fallen Giant* (Chicago: Contemporary Books, 1988), p. 63.
6. Peter Drucker, *Management: Tasks, Responsibilities, Practices* (New York: Perennial Library, 1974), p. 302.

CHAPTER 3

1. Richard Schonberger, *Building a Chain of Customers* (New York: Free Press, 1989).
2. Tom Peters, *Thriving on Chaos* (New York: Perennial Library, 1987).
3. Brian Dumaine, "Is Big Still Good?" *Fortune*, April 20, 1992, pp. 50-55.
4. Robert M. Tomasko, *Downsizing: Reshaping the Corporation of the Future* (New York: Amacom, 1987).
5. Kenichi Ohmae, "Planting for a Global Harvest," *Harvard Business Review*, July-August 1989, p. 136.

CHAPTER 4

1. Peter Krass, "New Kids on the Block," *Information Week*, August 26, 1991, p. 44.

2. *The Economist*, "The Computer Industry Runs out of Room," June 29, 1991, pp. 57-58.
3. Alvin Toffler, *The Third Wave* (New York: William Morrow, 1980).
4. Forrester Research, *The Computing Strategy Report*, February 1992.
5. Steven Milunovitch, CFA, *Downsizing!* (New York: Salomon Brothers, May 1991).
6. William Bulkeley, "PC Networks Begin to Oust Mainframes in Some Companies," *Wall Street Journal*, May 23, 1990, p. A1.
7. John Verity, "Rethinking the Computer," *Business Week*, November 26, 1990, pp. 116-125.

CHAPTER 5

1. Tom Parker, *In One Day* (Boston: Houghton Mifflin, 1984), p. 85.
2. Alyssa A. Lappen, "Follow Through: Back in Focus." *Forbes*, August 24, 1987, p.8.

CHAPTER 6

1. Tom Peters, "Want to Survive? Here Are 32 Places to Start," *New York Times*, February 11, 1992, p. C4.

CHAPTER 7

1. "ABB in Eastern Europe: Showing Promise," *The Economist*, June 29, 1991, pp. 61-62.

2. William Taylor, "The Logic of Global Business: An Interview with ABB's Percy Barnevik," *Harvard Business Review*, March-April 1991, p. 91.
3. William Peterson III, "Xerox Remakes Management," *Rochester Democrat and Chronicle*, January 18, 1991, pp. B1-3.
4. John McElroy, "Building Taurus: Inside Ford's (Crowded) Chicago Plant," *Automotive Industries*, May 1986, pp. 88-89.
5. "Appliance Production Highlight: Shifting into World Class Manufacturing," Dana Chase Publications, February 1990 (reprint).
6. Carol J. Loomis, "Can John Akers Save IBM?" *Fortune*, July 15, 1991, p. 56.
7. Peter Coy, "Twin Engines: Can Bob Allen Blend Computers and Telecommunications at AT&T?" *Business Week*, January 20, 1992, pp. 56-62.
8. William P. Barrett, "I Get a Kick Out of Seeing Something Being Made," *Forbes*, Feb. 5, 1990, pp. 96-97.
9. Ira Krepchin, "Advanced Systems: PC-based MRP, DRP Help Lipton Cut Inventories," *Modern Materials Handling*, February 1989, pp. 22-25.
10. Discussion with Herb McCauley.
11. Joseph A. Juran, "Quality Advisor: Made in USA," *Manufacturing Engineering*, April 1991, pp. 10-13.

CHAPTER 8

1. Joseph A. Juran, "Quality Advisor: Made in USA," *Manufacturing Engineering*, April 1991, pp. 10-13.

2. The list of quality attributes was partly created by David Garvin, Joseph Juran, and Philip Crosby, plus a few thoughts of my own.
3. Joseph A. Juran, ed. *Quality Control Handbook*, 3d ed. (New York: McGraw-Hill, 1974), p. 2.
4. David A. Garvin, *Managing Quality: The Strategic and Competitive Edge* (New York: Free Press, 1988). I am indebted to Garvin for much of the material on the history of quality.
5. Richard Schonberger, *Building a Chain of Customers* (New York: Free Press, 1989).
6. Richard T. Pascale, *Managing on the Edge: How the Smartest Companies Use Conflict to Stay Ahead* (New York: Simon & Schuster, 1990), p. 248.
7. Christopher Hart and Christopher Bogan, *The Baldrige: What It Is, How It's Won, and How It's Changing the Way America Does Business* (New York: McGraw-Hill, 1992).
8. Gary Spizizen, "The ISO 9000 Standards: Creating a Level Playing Field for International Quality," *National Productivity Review*, Spring 1992.
9. Ron Zemke, "Bashing the Baldrige," *Training*, February 1991, p. 30.
10. Tom Peters, *Thriving on Chaos* (New York: Perennial Library, 1987), pp. 70- 85.

CHAPTER 9

1. Attributed to William L. Bryan, "Other Comments," *Forbes*, June 10, 1991, p. 28.
2. Harvey A. Robbins, *Turf Wars: Moving from Competition to Collaboration* (Chicago: Scott Foresman, 1990). Adapted from an example.

EPILOG

1. Franck A. De Chambreau, "Keeping the Tall Ships Afloat," *Across the Board*, March 1987, pp. 54-57.
2. Carol J. Loomis, "Can John Akers Save IBM?" *Fortune*, July 15, 1991, p. 56.
3. Brian Dumaine, "Closing the Innovation Gap," *Fortune*, December 2, 1991, p. 58.
4. John Fucini with Susy Fucini, *Working for the Japanese: Inside Mazda's American Auto Plant* (New York: The Free Press, 1990), pp. 89-121.
5. James Fallows, *More Like Us* (Boston: Houghton Mifflin, 1989), p. ix.
6. Stephen S. Cohen and John Zysman, *Manufacturing Matters* (New York: Basic Books, 1987), pp. xi-xiv.
7. Peter Drucker, "The Emerging Theory of Manufacturing," *Harvard Business Review*, May June 1990, pp. 94-102.

Bibliography

"ABB in Eastern Europe: Showing Promise." *The Economist*, June 29, 1991, pp. 61-62.

Aguayo, Rafael. *Dr. Deming: The American Who Taught the Japanese About Quality*. (New York: Simon & Schuster, 1990).

Applegate, Lynda M., James I. Cash, Jr., and D. Quinn Mills. "Information Technology and Tomorrow's Manager." *Harvard Business Review*, November-December, 1988, pp. 128-137.

"Appliance Production Highlight: Shifting into World Class Manufacturing." Dana Chase Publications, February 1990 (reprint).

"At Last, Good News." *Business Week* (Editorial), June 3, 1991, pp. 24- 25.

Avery, Susan. "Don't Be So Fast with Moves that Decentralize the Purchasing Job." *Purchasing*, November 20, 1986, p. 31.

Baer, Arthur H., Jr. "Survival Lessons from a Divisional Manager." *Industry Week*, August 1, 1988, pp. 36-45.

Bailey, Nick E. "Why the Computer Is Altering Decentralized Management." *International Management*, June 1986, p. 79.

Barrett, William P. "I Get a Kick Out of Seeing Something Being Made." *Forbes*, February 5, 1990, pp. 96-97.

Barry, John A. *Technobabble*. (Cambridge: The MIT Press, 1991).

Bartlett, Brian. "The Bypassed Manager." *Management Today*, June 1987, pp. 82-84.

Bauer, Roy A., Emilio Collar, Victor Tang, and Patrick Houston. *The Silverlake Project: Transformation at IBM*. (New York: Oxford University Press, 1992).

Booker, Ellis. "Exploring Options for CIM."*Computer-World*, May 29, 1989, pp. 40-42.

Borrus, Amy. "Can Japan's Giants Cut the Apron Strings?" *Business Week*, May 14, 1990, pp. 105-106.

Bowles, Jerry and Joshua Hammond. *Beyond Quality: How 50 Winning Companies Use Continuous Improvement*. (New York: G.P. Putnam's Sons, 1991).

Brimelow, Peter and Gregory Viscusi. "Socialism by Another Name." *Forbes*, December 9, 1991, pp. 100-101.

Bryan, William L., attrib. "Other Comments." *Forbes*, June 10, 1991, p. 28.

Bulkeley, William. "PC Networks Begin To Oust Mainframes In Some Companies." *Wall Street Journal*, May 23, 1990, p. A1.

"Can We Improve Productivity?" *Management Accounting*, September 1991, p. 12.

Carlyle, Ralph Emmett. "Leading IS Shops Shifting to a Centralized Structure." *Datamation*, November 15, 1987, pp. 17-19.

"Centralising Again." *The Economist* (Editorial), August 13, 1988.

Cohen, Stephen S., and John Zysman. *Manufacturing Matters*. (New York: Basic Books, 1987).

Coleman, Fred. "Is Anyone Listening?" *Newsweek*, April 22, 1991, pp. 35-36.

"The Computer Industry Runs Out of Room." *The Economist*, June 29, 1991, pp. 57-58.

Cook, Brian M. "In Search of Six Sigma: 99.9997% Defect Free." *Industry Week*, October 1, 1990, pp. 60-65.

Coy, Peter. "Twin Engines: Can Bob Allen Blend Computers and Telecommunications at AT&T?" *Business Week*, January 20, 1992, pp. 56-62.

Crosby, Philip. *Quality Is Free*. (New York: Penguin Books, 1979).

De Chambreau, Franck A. "Keeping the Tall Ships Afloat." *Across the Board*, March 1987, p. 54-57.

Dent, Harry S., Jr. "Corporation of the Future: How Strategic Alliances and Networking Will Reshape the 90s." *Small Business Reports*, May, 1990, pp. 54-63.

Detouzos, Michael, Richard Lester, Robert Solow, and the MIT Commission. *Made in America: Regaining the Productive Edge*. (Cambridge: MIT Press, 1989).

Dobyns, Lloyd, and Clare Crawford-Mason. *Quality or Else: The Revolution in World Business*. (Boston: Houghton Mifflin, 1991).

Drucker, Peter. "The Emerging Theory of Manufacturing." *Harvard Business Review*, May/June 1990, pp. 94-102.

—-. *Management: Tasks, Responsibilities, Practices*. (New York: Perennial Library, 1974).

"The Dynamics of 'Rightsizing.'" Los Angeles: Nantucket Corporation, 1991 (brochure).

Dumaine, Brian. "Closing the Innovation Gap." *Fortune*, December 2, 1991, p. 58.

—-. "Is Big Still Good?" *Fortune*, April 20, 1992, pp. 50-55.

Eisenstodt, Gale and Amy Feldman. “Sharply Focused.” *Forbes*, December 24, 1990, p. 50-53.

Eskow, Dennis. “Kodak Blazes Corporate Path by Farming Out IS Support.” *PC Week*, August 21, 1989, pp. 1, 6.

—-. “Kodak's IS Chief Represents New Generation,” *PC Week*, August 21, 1989, p. 6.

Fallows, James. *More Like Us*. (Boston: Houghton Mifflin, 1989).

Forrester Research, Inc. “Software: A Global View.” *The Software Strategy Report*. Cambridge: October, 1991.

—-. *The Computing Strategy Report*. Cambridge: February, 1992.

Fucini, John, with Susy Fucini. *Working for the Japanese: Inside Mazda's American Auto Plant*. (New York: The Free Press, 1990), pp. 89-121.

Gabor, Andrea. “Overseas Operators: Taking Stock.” *U.S. News & World Report*, January 15, 1990, p. 44.

Gall, Adrienne, ed. “How Does Decentralization Affect Human Resource Departments?” *Training and Development Journal*, February 1987, pp. 20-24.

Garvin, David A. *Managing Quality: The Strategic and Competitive Edge*. (New York: Free Press, 1988).

Gautschi, T.F. “Kodak Tackles Shorter Design Times.” *Design News*, June 25, 1990, p. 200.

Gelb, Leslie. “Whining, Excuses, Hysteria.” *New York Times*, June 23, 1991, p. E15.

Gordon, Bernard K. “The Vanishing Trade Deficit.” *Wall Street Journal*, May 28, 1991, p. A18.

Halberstam, David. *The Reckoning*. New York: William Morrow, 1986.

Harmon, Roy L. and Leroy D. Peterson. “Reinventing the Factory.” *Across the Board*, March 1990, pp. 30-37.

Hart, Christopher, and Christopher Bogan. *The Baldrige: What It Is, How It's Won, and How It's Changing the Way America Does Business.* (New York: McGraw-Hill, 1992).

Hayes, Robert H, and Steven C. Wheelwright. *Restoring Our Competitive Edge.* (New York: John Wiley & Sons, 1990).

Heidke, Ronald L. "'New IE Excellence' Program Is Working at Kodak." *Industrial Engineering*, August 1989, pp. 40-45.

Hellenack, Les. "The Trend Toward Decentralization and Downsizing: Eastman Kodak's Experience." *New Software Technologies.* (Framingham, MA: International Data Corporation, August 1989).

Hennessy, Edward L., Jr. "Back to Basics." *Industry Week*, November 20, 1989, p. 23.

Horwitt, Elizabeth. "Kodak Training IS on Server Strategy." *ComputerWorld*, July 24, 1989, pp. 1, 101.

Houston, Patrick. "High Anxiety." *Business Month*, June 1990, pp. 32-41.

Hubben, Herbert. "The Haunted Headquarters." *Across the Board*, January 1990, p. 64.

Hudson, Richard L. "IBM Again Revamps European Sector." *Wall Street Journal*, April 22, 1991, p. B3A.

IDS Financial Services, Inc. "Computers: Network News Is the Talk of the Industry." *West of Wall Street*, February 22, 1991, p. 3.

Imai, Masaaki. *Kaizen: The Key to Japan's Competitive Success.* (New York: Random House, 1986.)

"Increasing Margins: Three Production Criteria to Arm Plant Managers in Their Shift to JIT," *Manufacturing Executive's Report*, August 1990, pp. 1-12.

Isenberg-O'Laughlin, Jo. "Poised for the 90's: The Re-Making of American Manufacturing." National Association of Manufacturers, Advertising Supplement. *Industry Week*, February 6, 1990, pp. S1-S18.

Ishiharo, Shintaro, and Akio Morita. *The Japan That Can Say No* (trans. Frank Baldwin). (New York: Simon & Schuster, 1990).

Juran, Joseph A. "Quality Advisor: Made in USA." *Manufacturing Engineering*, April 1991, pp. 10-13.

Juran, Joseph A., ed. *Quality Control Handbook*. 3d ed. (New York: McGraw-Hill, 1974), p. 2.

Kennedy, Paul. *The Rise and Fall of the Great Powers*. (New York: Random House, 1987), p. 23.

King, John Leslie. "Centralized versus Decentralized Computing." *Computing Surveys*, Vol. 15, No. 4, December 1983, pp. 319-349.

Klein, Janice. "The Human Cost of Manufacturing Reform."*Harvard Business Review*, March-April 1989, pp. 60-66.

Klein, Theodore P. "How to Avoid the Five Biggest Downsizing Errors." *ComputerWorld*, June 11, 1990, pp. 91-92.

"Kodak Manager Represents a New Generation." *PC Week* (Editorial), August 21, 1989, p. 84.

Krass, Peter. "New Kids on the Block." *Information Week* August 26, 1991, p. 44.

Krepchin, Ira. "Advanced Systems: PC-based MRP, DRP Help Lipton Cut Inventories." *Modern Materials Handling*, February 1989, pp. 22-25.

La Belle, Antoinette and H. Edward Nye. "Whither the IT Organization?" *Sloan Management Review*, Summer 1987, pp. 75-77.

Lappen, Alyssa A. "Follow Through: Back in Focus." *Forbes*, August 24, 1987, p. 8.

Lareau, William. *American Samurai: Warrior for the Coming Dark Ages of American Business*. (Clinton, NJ: New Win Publishing, 1991).

Lee, Albert. *Call Me Roger: The Story of How Roger Smith, Chairman of General Motors, Transformed the Industrial Leader into a Fallen Giant.* (Chicago: Contemporary Books, 1988).

Loomis, Carol J. "Can John Akers Save IBM?" *Fortune*, July 15, 1991, p. 56.

"Making Micros Work." *Manufacturing Systems*, September 1986, pp. 31-32.

Main, Jeremy. "Manufacturing the Right Way." *Fortune*, May 21, 1990, p. 54.

Mandell, Mel. "Corporate Computers: How Necessary?" *Across the Board*, March, 1991, pp. 50-54.

"Manufacturing Excellence is JRP." (Presentation) Minneapolis: FOURTH SHIFT Corporation, 1991.

McCormick, John J. "Bottom Line on Client-Server." *Information Week*, January 20, 1992, p. 6.

McElroy, John. "Building Taurus: Inside Ford's (Crowded) Chicago Plant." *Automotive Industries*, May 1986, pp. 88-89.

McKenna, Joseph F. "Smart Scarecrows: The Wizardry of Empowerment." *Industry Week*, July 16, 1990, pp. 8-19.

MicroDesign Resources, Inc. "Microprocessor Forecast for 1991 and Beyond." *Microprocessor Report*, Sebastopol, CA, p. 1.

Milbank, Dana. "Dying Breed: No Glamour, No Glory, Being a Manufacturer Today Can Take Guts." *Wall Street Journal*, June 3, 1991, p. 1.

Miller, William H. "Industry's 92 Challenges." *Industry Week*, January 6, 1992, p. 13.

Milunovitch, Steven, CFA. "Downsizing!" Salomon Brothers, Inc., May 1991.

Mitchell, Russell. "How Ford Hit the Bull's-Eye with Taurus." *Business Week*, June 30, 1986, pp. 69-70.

Modic, Stanley J. "Motivating Without Promotions." *Industry Week*, June 19, 1989, pp. 24-27.

Moskowitz, Milton, Robert Levering, and Michael Katz. *Everybody's Business*. (New York: Doubleday, 1990).

Musich, Paula. "LAN Takes Center Stage in New Kodak EDI System." *PC Week*, April 2, 1990, pp. 1, 8.

"Too Many Computers Spoil the Broth." The Economist, August 24, 1991, p. 30.

'92 RMA Annual Statement Studies. Robert Morris Associates, 1992.

Noaker, Paula M. "The 'Demassification' Solution." *Production*, July 1989, pp. 72-74.

Ohmae, Kenichi. "Planting for a Global Harvest." *Harvard Business Review*, July-August 1989, p. 136.

O'Reilly, Brian. "Preparing For Leaner Times." *Fortune*, January 27, 1992, pp. 40-41.

"Outsourcing Revisited." Alex Brown & Sons, Computer Services Group, October 14, 1991.

Parker, Tom. *In One Day*. (Boston: Houghton Mifflin, 1984), p. 85.

Pascale, Richard T. *Managing on the Edge: How the Smartest Companies Use Conflict to Stay Ahead*. (New York: Simon & Schuster, 1990), p. 248.

"PC Invaders Gain Stronghold in Manufacturing." *Industrial Computing*, March/April 1990, pp. 40-42.

Peters, Tom. "The Destruction of Hierarchy." *Industry Week*, August 15, 1988, pp. 33-35.

—-. *Thriving on Chaos*. (New York: Perennial Library, 1987).

—-. "Want to Survive? Here Are 32 Places to Start." *New York Times*, February 11, 1992, p. C4.

Peterson, William III. "Xerox Remakes Management." *Rochester Democrat and Chronicle*, January 18, 1991, pp. B1-3.

Powell, Bill. "Tips for the Hands-Off CEO." *Newsweek*, March 16, 1987, p. 52.

Pringle, Charles D. "Seven Reasons Why Managers Don't Delegate." *Management Solutions*, November 1986, pp. 26-30.

"A Revolution of Pure Light." *San Francisco Examiner*, July 7, 1991, p. D14.

Rigdon, Joan E. "Kodak Tries to Prepare for Filmless Era Without Inviting Demise of Core Business." *Wall Street Journal*, April 18, 1991, p. B1.

Robbins, Harvey A. *Turf Wars: Moving from Competition to Collaboration.* (Chicago: Scott Foresman, 1990).

Schlesinger, Jacob M. "Future Appears Bright for Flash Chips." *Wall Street Journal*, p. B1.

Schonberger, Richard. *Building a Chain of Customers.* (New York: Free Press, 1989).

—. "'Customer Chains': Links to Survival." *Industry Week*, April 16, 1990, pp. 27-32.

Sewell, Alan. "Departmental Computing: Distributing the Power." *Datamation*, October 15, 1987, pp. 82-94

Shackney, Orry Y. and Robert J. Cecil. "IE's Training Makes Them Effective Users of Rightsizing for Organizational Renewal." *Industrial Engineering*, March 1989, pp. 20-22.

Sheridan, John H. "Lessons from the Gurus." *Industry Week*, August 6, 1990, pp. 35-41.

—. "MRP II: Still a Sound Control Strategy?" *Industry Week*, July 3, 1989, pp. 39-45.

—. "World-Class Manufacturing." *Industry Week*, July 2, 1990, pp. 36- 46.

Spizizen, Gary. "The ISO 9000 Standards: Creating a Level Playing Field for International Quality." *National Productivity Review*, Spring 1992.

"State of the I/S Union." *Computer Decisions*, February 1989, pp. 52-57.

Stuckey, M.M. "Demassification: A Cost Comparison of Micro vs Mini." *Future Thinker*, September 7, 1989, pp. 11-13.

—-. *Demassification: A Cost Comparison of Micro vs Mini*. Microtechnology Investments Publishing, 1989.

Taylor, Alex III. "Can GM Remodel itself?" *Fortune*, January 13, 1992, pp. 26-35.

Taylor, William. "The Logic of Global Business: An Interview with ABB's Percy Barnevik." *Harvard Business Review*, March-April 1991, p. 91.

Tereske, John. "Make Or Buy: Now It's a Data-Processing Question, Too." *Industry Week*, July 16, 1990, pp. 54-56.

Therrien, Lois. "The Upstarts Teaching McDonalds a Thing or Two." *Business Week*, October 21, 1991, p. 122.

Thomas, Philip. *Competitiveness Through Total Cycle Time*. (New York: McGraw-Hill, 1990).

Toffler, Alvin. *The Third Wave*. (New York: William Morrow, 1980).

Tomasko, Robert M. *Downsizing: Reshaping the Corporation of the Future*. (New York: Amacom, 1987).

Tovar, Roberta T., Allison Rossett, and Nancy Carter. "Centralized Training in a Decentralized Organization." *Training and Development Journal*, February 1989, pp. 62-65.

Trespasz, Nancy, and Ann Stevens. "Mainframes Being Put Out to Pasture." *Computer Reseller News*, June 18, 1990.

Verespej, Michael A. "Sidney Harman's Message: We Need More Manufacturers, Not Pretenders." *Industry Week*, February 6, 1989, pp. 16-18.

Verity, John. "Rethinking the Computer." *Business Week*, November 26, 1990, pp. 116-125.

Walker, Alfred J. "Human Resources: Preparing for the Next Century." *Personnel Journal*, November 1987, pp.

106-112.

Walton, Mary. *The Deming Management Method.* (New York: Putnam, 1986).

Walton, Richard E. "From Control to Commitment in the Marketplace." *Harvard Business Journal*, March-April, 1985, p. 77.

Watson, Thomas J., Jr. *Father Son & Co.* (New York: Bantam Books, 1990).

Wight, Oliver W. *Production and Inventory Management in the Computer Age*. (Boston: CBI, 1981).

Wilder, Clinton. "Fear of the 'O' Word." *ComputerWorld*, February 5, 1990, p. 85.

World Economic Forum and IMD International. *World Competitiveness Report*. 10th and 11th eds. Lausanne: 1991, 1992.

Zemke, Ron. "Bashing the Baldrige." *Training*, February 1991, p. 30.

Zuckerman, Morton B. "George Herbert (Hoover) Bush." (Editorial) *U.S. News & World Report*, January 20, 1992, p. 68.

About the Author

M.M. Stuckey is the founder and CEO of FOURTH SHIFT Corporation, a company that creates, makes, and markets manufacturing management, client/server software and systems. Mr. Stuckey has held executive positions in two *Fortune* 500 companies and has been president of a large high-tech manufacturing company. He is one of America's foremost proponents of corporate demassification, a term he coined. He is the author of numerous books and articles.

Index

OTHER BOOKS FROM PRODUCTIVITY PRESS

Productivity Press publishes and distributes materials on continuous improvement in productivity, quality, and the creative involvement of all employees. Many of our products are direct source materials from Japan that have been translated into English for the first time and are available exclusively from Productivity. Supplemental products and services include membership groups, conferences, seminars, in-house training and consulting, audio-visual training programs, and industrial study missions. Call toll-free 1-800-394-6868 for our free catalog.

Vision Management
Translating Strategy into Action

SANNO Management Development Research Center (ed.)

For over ten years, managers of Japan's top companies have gathered at SANNO University to brainstorm about innovative corporate management methods. This book is based on the proven methodology that evolved from their ideas. It describes how the intangible aspects of vision-based strategy can be integrated into a concrete implementation model and clarifies the relationship among vision, strategy, objectives, goals, and day-to-day activities.
ISBN 0-915299-80-1 / 272 pages / $29.95 / Order VISM-B209

Technoshifts
Meeting the Challenge of Technological Change

Smaïl Aït-El-Hadj

Technoshifts presents a broad perspective of the phenomenon of ongoing technological advancement and the corporate mentality and organization necessary to respond to it most effectively. More than a theoretical discussion, it examines the recent shift in industrial, mechanical, and electro-mechanical technologies and offers a concrete analysis to help you recognize the indicators of future shifts and use new technologies to the utmost advantage.
ISBN 0-915299-83-6 / 224 pages / $34.95 / Order TECHNO-B209

Hoshin Kanri
Policy Deployment for Successful TQM

Yoji Akao (ed.)

Hoshin kanri, the Japanese term for policy deployment, is an approach to strategic planning and quality improvement that has become a pillar of total quality management (TQM) for a growing number of U.S. firms. This book is a compilation of examples of policy deployment that demonstrates how company vision is converted into individual responsibility. It includes practical guidelines, 150 charts and diagrams, and five case studies that illustrate the procedures of hoshin kanri. The six steps to advanced process planning are reviewed and include a five-year vision, one-year plan, deployment to departments, execution, monthly audit, and annual audit.

ISBN 0-915299-57-7 / 256 pages / $54.95 / Order HOSHIN-B209

Workplace Management

Taiichi Ohno

An in-depth view of how one of this century's leading industrial thinkers approaches problem solving and continuous improvement. Gleaned from Ohno's forty years of experimentation and innovation at Toyota, where he created just-in-time (JIT), this book explains the concepts Ohno considered most important to successful top management, with an emphasis on quality.

ISBN 0-915299-19-4 / 165 pages / $39.95 / Order WPM-B209

Championship Management
An Action Model for High Performance

James A. Belohlav

Many books extol the values of being an excellent company; this one goes beyond to explain how excellence can be achieved and why it is so critically important. A model for action demonstrates how any company can become a championship-caliber company. Further, it explains why some excellent companies lose their edge, while others remain excellent, and why still others appear to be excellent but are not.

ISBN 0-915299-76-3 / 272 pages / $29.95 / Order CHAMPS-B209

Managerial Engineering
Techniques for Improving Quality and Productivity in the Workplace

Ryuji Fukuda

A proven path to managerial success, based on reliable methods developed by one of Japan's leading productivity experts and winner of the coveted Deming Prize for quality. Dr. W. Edwards Deming, world-famous consultant on quality, says that the book "provides an excellent and clear description of the devotion and methods of Japanese management to continual improvement of quality." (Training programs on CEDAC, the award-winning system outlined in this book, are also available from Productivity.)

ISBN 0-915299-09-7 / 208 pages / $44.95 / Order ME-B209

Canon Production System
Creative Involvement of the Total Workforce

compiled by the Japan Management Association

A fantastic success story! Canon set a goal to increase productivity by three percent per month and achieved it! The first book-length case study to show how to combine the most effective Japanese management principles and quality improvement techniques into one overall strategy that improves every area of the company on a continual basis.

ISBN 0-915299-06-2 / 256 pages / $39.95 / Order CANON-B209

Measuring, Managing, and Maximizing Performance

Will Kaydos

You do not need to be an exceptionally skilled technician or inspirational leader to improve your company's quality and productivity. In nontechnical, jargon-free, practical terms this book details the entire process of improving performance, from why and how the improvement process works to what must be done to begin and to sustain continuous improvement of performance. Special emphasis is given to the role that performance measurement plays in identifying problems and opportunities.

ISBN 0-915299-98-4 / 304 pages / $39.95 Order MMMP-B209